The Wee Book – Bei
Faith – Fellowship –

The Wee Book

Being Sober

Eddie Mackay

My Three Lives

Alcoholism – Discovery - Recovery

The Wee Book – Being Sober

Life is but a day at most – (Robert Burns 1788)

This quote from our Ayrshire Bard helped me Make it through another day of abstinence in Early Recovery. When attending my first A.A. meetings, members would provide encouragement by saying, "One Day at A Time" or "Just for Today." This prompted my recollection of that quote from Burns I had heard as a youngster. It worked for me on numerous occasions.

Disclaimer: - All views and opinions expressed in this life story are strictly personal. They do not represent the opinions of any entity with which I have been or may be affiliated.

Copyright ©2020 Eddie Mackay

All Rights reserved

ISBN - 9798682468775

Alcoholism – Discovery - Recovery

The Wee Book – Being Sober

Introduction

Being Eddie Mackay, an engineer come, livestock farmer, I have never authored anything other than engineering papers before this book. Always willing to speak about my sober life, I will now attempt to compose my story of **"Life in Recovery."** Having been born in Scotland on February 29th, 1936, I may be compared to Frederic in Gilbert and Sullivan`s Pirates of Penzance as A Paradox, A Paradox, A Most Ingenious Paradox. Unlike Frederic, however, I did celebrate the actual 21st anniversary of my birth on February 29th, 2020. I was well known and recognized for many years in the automotive world of aluminum truck body engineering, with numerous accomplishments and successes. Currently, I am known and recognized as a breeder of Scottish Highland Cattle. Also known for my continuous efforts in carrying a message of hope to the recovery community of Southwest Michigan. Hopefully, this book will be useful in putting a positive face on the many recovered alcoholics and addicts.

The Wee Book – Being Sober

Contents
Faith – Fellowship – Service - i
Life is but a day at most – (Robert Burns 1788) ii
Introduction iii
Acknowledgments vi
Chapter 1 – Our Stories Disclose in a General Way – 1
Chapter 2 – Another Blackout - 2
Chapter 3 – A Corporate Intervention - 3
Chapter 4 – Hazelden is Discovery – 9
Chapter 5 – Patricia's Death – 11
Chapter 6 – The Tiebout Unit – 14
Chapter 7 – Introduction to Alcoholics Anonymous - 18
Chapter 8 – Traveling in Early Recovery- 21
Chapter 9 - My First Tiebout Reunion - 23
Chapter 10 – Finding Sobriety - 27
Chapter 11 – Changing Vocation - 31
Chapter 12 – Living in Sobriety - 34
Chapter 13 – Service in Alcoholics Anonymous - 37
Chapter 14 – Becoming a Livestock Farmer - 39
Chapter 15 – My Young Life and Scottish Heritage– 41
Chapter 16 - Having a Genetic Propensity - 50
Chapter 17 – A New Immigrant – 51
Chapter 18 – The United States Army – 53
Chapter 19 – Truck Body Engineering - 55
Chapter 20 – The Making of a Package Car – 62
Chapter 21 – Advancements at Grumman - 67
Chapter 22 – New Products, Marriage, and Travels - 68
Chapter 23 - Dundonald Farm – 70

The Wee Book – Being Sober

Chapter 24 - Progressive Alcoholism - 72
Chapter 25 – U. S. Post Office Electric Vehicles - 74
Chapter 26 - Diesel Minivan to Long Life Vehicle 76
Chapter 27 - More Product and More Alcohol - 82
Chapter 28 - The Deutsche Bundespost – 84
Chapter 29 - Travelling in Early Abstinence - 87
Chapter 30 – Farming Life and Contented Sobriety 90
Chapter 31 - Farming and Conservation - 96
Chapter 32 - Continue – Continue – Continue - 99
Chapter 33 - Health Issues and Bounce Back – 106
Chapter 34 - 2020 Another Leap Year - 107
Chapter 35 - The Twelve Steps Process of Living - 109
Eulogy for Eddie Mackay - 122
About the Author - 123

The Wee Book – Being Sober

Acknowledgments

As Eddie Mackay, recovered alcoholic and child of God, I have authored this book. I am solely responsible for its content. The opinions, observations, and suggestions are based on my 26 years of experience with contented sobriety. Many of the quotes came from members of Alcoholics Anonymous. I do wish to express my gratitude to the great fellowship of Alcoholics Anonymous and the Twelve Step Process of Life, without which this book would not have been possible. I also express my thanks to my good friend Larry Koch for his guidance and suggestions. I am hopeful this story I am telling will carry a message of hope to anyone considering or continuing life in Recovery. I trust it will be useful, with maybe prompting some to smile.

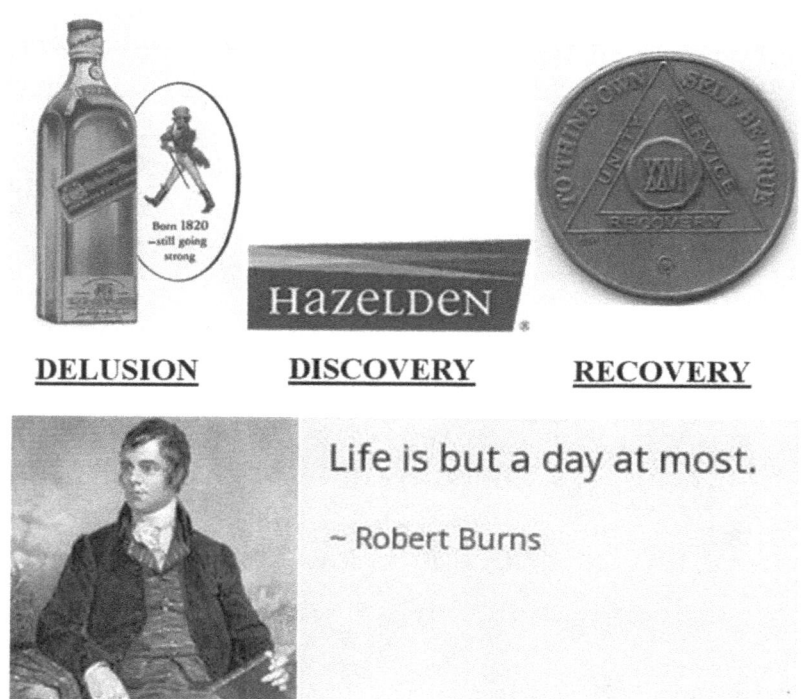

DELUSION   **DISCOVERY**   **RECOVERY**

Life is but a day at most.

~ Robert Burns

Alcoholism – Discovery - Recovery

Chapter 1 – Our Stories Disclose in a General Way –

Alcoholics Anonymous encourages the sharing of our many stories in a general way. Not necessarily too specific. The format typically describes *"what we used to be like" – "what happened"* – and *"what we are like now." - What did I used to be like?-* Had I thought I may write about me, I could have taken notes. As a blackout drinker, many of the stories told about me are purely hearsay. I did have many years of moderate drinking before the progression of chronic alcoholism and a destructive way of life. Considered by many to be a talented and productive engineer, I was fortunate to survive that alcoholic, delusional lifestyle. So,- *What happened?-* It certainly was not my doing! It can best be described as a Corporate Intervention. This would result in the *Discovery at Hazelden and Recovery at Alcoholics Anonymous,* bringing about a new way of life, including contented sobriety. *What am I like now?-* Today, I am a successful livestock farmer raising Scottish Highland Cattle and Cheviot Sheep. Blessed each new day to maintain an attitude of gratitude for just being sober. I do my best each day while trying to be useful to others. I carry a message of hope each week to inmates in the Saint Joseph County Jail in Centreville and the Michigan State Prison in Coldwater. As I consider how best to share this story, I feel that I have experienced three separate and distinctive lives. My first life involved being born, raised, and educated in Scotland. A second life being spent mostly as a productive and successful engineer in the United States of America. This also being the life when I would experience the progression of my alcoholism, leading to a corporate intervention. My third and ongoing life as a livestock farmer and an active member of the recovery community. Those years in Scotland were the *"Early Years."* From my arrival in the United States in June 1957, would be the *"Active Years."* A brief period of close to a year can only be described as *The Intervention and La-La Land."* The third and current life being *"Recovery."* Living in the recovery community has provided many blessings, never imagined.

Chapter 2 – Another Blackout -

It was Friday, August 13th of 1993, and I am not usually superstitious. Having left work for lunch earlier in the day, it had become an extended drinking lunch at the Eagles Club in Sturgis, Michigan. I was seemingly headed home to Three Rivers and had been driving in a blackout. Not on my usual route home, but driving on one of the many back roads. I should have been returning to work after lunch. I have no explanation for why I had not returned to work as usual. I do recall the flashing lights of the Sheriff car behind me, and I pulled my truck over. Previous experiences had evidenced a temporary cure for blackouts was blue and red flashing lights. Not my first such event! Presenting my license as requested and going through the actions of the sobriety test, such as walking the line and doing the alphabet, was no problem.

The young deputy said I smelled strongly of alcohol, and suggested I follow him to the Sheriff's Office as it was only a few miles, so I complied. The breathalyzer test indicated a BAC of 0.24, which resulted in immediate incarceration. Remembering that I had a Saturday business meeting, I used my influence to be released earlier than the required minimum of 24 hours. Also, before reaching a BAC of 0.04 as was a standard requirement. Just one more event in the life of this active and progressive alcoholic.

I was bothered much more than usual, having no explanation for where I was driving at the time of my arrest. No doubt, I had been creative with whatever I told the deputy. Being troubled by one more blackout was still no reason to consider that I quit drinking. It was just another scary event, happening with increased frequency. The increase in numbers and the duration of my blackouts were progressive. The alcoholic blackouts were becoming more bothersome than I wanted to admit—another expensive lawyer. With work done behind the scenes, the sentence was reasonable. Sentenced in October to spend four weekends in jail, sixty days license revocation, and eighteen months of restricted driver's license and fines. While this was another embarrassing and scary event, my drinking way of life continued as usual.

Not a reason for any reduction in my ongoing daily drinking routine. With travel being required in my routine business, I was prepared for the period of having a restricted license. One cannot rent a car from major car rental agencies using a driver's license with restrictions. I possessed two valid copies of my Michigan Driver license, along with a current New York Driver License. Always prepared for my routine life of travel in the U.S. and overseas. I minimized my local driving temporarily but certainly did not quit. I had a friend drive me each evening to the bar since both my car and truck were well known by all local law enforcement agencies. I did also continue to have my daily drinks for lunch with the good old boys.

CRASH MACKAY

This crash helmet was presented by the headquarters staff of Grumman Olson on my 25th anniversary in 1986. Recognition of my driving in alcoholic blackouts on so many occasions. Destroying so many vehicles, and often with significant bodily injury to myself. Fortunate never to have caused harm to any other individual. I did lots of damage to mailboxes, trees, fences, and vehicles. The ***"Guardian Angels"*** certainly protected me

Chapter 3 – A Corporate Intervention -

In addition to my tasks required as V.P. of Engineering at Grumman Olson, I had become a member of the Grumman Corporation Litigation Team. We would meet monthly at the Grumman Headquarters in Bethpage Long Island, NY. Typically reviewing ongoing litigation involving the subsidiaries of The Grumman Corporation. When I arrived at headquarters, a friend wanted to discuss my arrest. The President of Grumman had instructed this lawyer friend to have me get involved with two individuals in Human Resources. These fellows supposedly had lots of experience in matters relative to drugs and alcohol. Assuring this friend that all was resolved with the court, I did agree. to a 6-30 am Tuesday meeting with these two individuals before the regular workday.

 I knew both these fellows, having met them on previous occasions when Grumman initiated employee drug testing in the various subsidiaries. Part of their effort involved teaching supervisors on how to handle employees with apparent drug or alcohol problems. The company provided outside counseling at no cost to the employee. I did have some experience with this counseling service with one of my engineers. I never considered such problems would be associated with someone like myself. We had a good serious discussion about my recent and previous arrests for allegedly driving under the influence (DUI), and how I had handled them legally, without serious outcomes. They were only aware of a few such problems. I had no reason to enlighten them as to the real number and frequency. Their main concern seemed to be the new Michigan law that considered third offense DUI. A felony as opposed to a misdemeanor. If convicted as a felon, I could not remain a corporate officer of Grumman. I found it easy to discuss my ongoing heavy drinking with these fellows, even admitting to having experienced blackouts and vehicle wrecks. The number and severity of those events were minimized. Never known to miss work being one of my great strengths, and being in Michigan, it was easy to minimize my daily consumption of alcohol.

The Increased bodyweight was evident, having been noted and discussed as part of my annual physical exam, which was required of all corporate officers. There was no doubt I looked like a heavy drinker. Unaware at this time just how many individuals these fellows had assisted, they did seem familiar with alcoholism. I was not defensive, admitting that I did want to get some control over my excessive drinking. I was not considering quitting entirely. Our conversations seemed relatively free and comfortable since they already seemed to know quite a lot about me. I could not hide the increased body weight caused by my drinking, along with my bright red nose. One of my truck engineering friends compared Mackay`s nose to a chimsel. The automotive abbreviation CHMSL referred to Center High Mounted Stop Light, and it seemed an apt description for my red nose. We had joked about it frequently.

These human resource fellows suggested I enter a facility on Long Island for evaluation and assessment. I rejected that idea immediately. They would then suggest that I consider a facility nearer to my residence. They claimed that a facility called Hazelden was one of the best, and close to my home. It was agreed that I would give this suggestion serious consideration, mainly due to the grave concern of the President of Grumman. This President had always shown a particular liking for me. I did agree to a meeting with these fellows at 6-30 am the following morning to continue our discussion. When leaving their office to get on with regular business, I heard one fellow say, *"Try it, Eddie, what have you got to lose"*? Our meeting on litigation and business matters went exceptionally well, allowing me to catch a late flight back to Detroit, eliminating another overnight on Long Island.

The trip from New York`s La Guardia to Detroit Metro was a typical two drink flight that I had flown frequently. While drinking my Scotch, it seemed there was a *"wee fellow"* sitting on my shoulder saying, *"Try it, Eddie, what have you got to lose."* The voice was repetitious. I recall that constant voice in my ear while I sipped my drink. Arriving in my office early on Wednesday morning, I made a direct call to the office of those two individuals located in the basement of Grumman Headquarters. The one who answered immediately asked why I had missed our scheduled 6-30 am meeting. I informed him that I was back in my Michigan office doing real engineering work. He was not at all pleased that I had missed that meeting. It seemed he had been tasked with providing the President of Grumman with the outcome of our discussion. I eased his by concerns when telling him I would willingly make the visit to Hazelden since it was supposedly in my area. Being from New York, it seems they could not differentiate between Michigan and Minnesota, as Hazelden was 650 miles northwest of my home. He did seem relieved when hearing my acceptance of his suggestion. He proceeded to give me a telephone number for Hazelden. He also provided a unique insurance coverage number, recognizable by whomever I spoke with at Hazelden.

Having assumed he would make the necessary arrangements, I suggested he do that. He then told me quite bluntly to *"Make the Call,"* and he hung up. This was taken as an insult to a perceived prestigious Vice President. He was ensuring that I was the one deciding to go to Hazelden. Making that call at what was 6-30 am in Minnesota, I was informed that a telephone interview at 9.00 am would be required to provide my personal information. Now I began to wonder what I was getting involved in. This caused me some anxiety, making me feel quite nervous, which was not usual.

After the telephone interview, discussing my physical condition and drinking habits, this proficient woman informed me that I could be admitted to Hazelden within two to three weeks. Being *"my usual arrogant self,"* I responded, *"If you cannot get this handled within a week, then just forget it."* She said she would discuss this with her supervisor, promising to call me back the next day. On Thursday, November 4[th,] this nice, polite woman called as promised, providing me with instructions for arrival at Hazelden on November 10th. Informing me to be prepared for what may be a 28-day stay. That news did not sit well, but I decided to go with the flow. I proceeded to make the arrangements for my absence from my engineering work, including having someone take care of my old farm. Then I informed the President of Grumman Olson, who seemed thrilled with this crazy idea. He stated that I would be considered to be on a particular assignment to avoid any concerns. I informed my secretary and another close friend that had traveled with me in Europe. I also needed to tell my stepdaughter, who also worked at Grumman Olson. She seemed thrilled with the idea. I then arranged for a good friend to be the caretaker of the farm with my few sheep. I had no idea what I was getting myself involved in. I would not back off after having made the decision. Those few days, until I departed for Hazelden, were not easy, and no doubt, my alcohol consumption increased. My head was in turmoil.

On November 10th, a close friend, a "West by God Virginia Hillbilly," took me to Kalamazoo airport for the 7.00 am flight to Minneapolis/St Paul. I finished off a bottle of Johnnie Red along the way. I had not slept but tried to act as if all was normal. I was nervous and confused about what I was doing. On arrival at the Minneapolis airport, I did as had been instructed, going to a specified pick- up location. No one would show up as promised. In those days, there were still public telephones on the wall, so I made a call, being informed the driver was delayed. He was still scheduled to pick me up, with anticipated arrival shortly. Telling that woman that I would be in the bar, that is where I headed. There were few customers in the bar at that early hour. Being one of only three, and that was alright.

Finishing my first drink, and about to order a refill, when an older fellow walked in. He approached and asked if I was Eddie Mackay? He had no problem picking me out of the three customers. We headed off on that fifty miles trip to Center City. My driver, a retiree who did pickups as a part-time job, was also a longtime member of Alcoholics Anonymous. He did his best with encouragement, sharing stories of the many people he had picked up that had met success in Recovery. He also provided me with some idea of what to expect upon arrival. I was processed through the medical unit of Hazelden called Ignatia.

After a few questions, I was subjected to a thorough physical examination. Then required to complete an extensive questionnaire with pertinent questions about my drinking history and habits.

Proceeding to describe my drinking history as, first 10 years, second ten years, third ten years, and last ten years to the doctor, she would ask if I drank all my life? I was quick to respond, *"Not Yet, Ma`am."* My casual description of those first ten years referred to my beer drinking in the village pubs, with binges on weekends and drinking as much beer as we could afford. Then becoming a daily drinker in America with heavy drinking on the weekend ski trips. My army years with sporadic beer binges, and the switch from beer to Scotch Whisky after leaving the army. My second ten years were described as continued daily drinking, mostly in moderate amounts, with some heavy weekend drinking. These years also involved business travels with increased consumption and some problems with law enforcement, but no serious consequences. The third ten years was when my daily amounts increased, mostly what I consumed on business events and travels. More problems occurred with law enforcement and more consequences, although still manageable. The fourth and last ten years was when my physical problems began, with an increase in weight, and the nosebleeds, etc. The alcoholic blackouts were occurring more frequently and with longer duration. I would never be honest about my blackouts until well along in my Recovery. I had a convenient lapse of memory about anything problematic. My alcoholism had progressed even though I overlooked the changes in me. Now loaded up with Librium, I was informed that I would remain in the medical unit overnight. Then assigned to a unit if all seemed well. I wanted to know how long this assessment would take, and when I would be returning home. When informed to anticipate a 28-day stay, that did not sit well, and I expressed my negative feelings. They showed no concern with my impatient attitude. No doubt, having processed many others just like me. The next morning, I was assigned to a unit. Along with a newcomer named Bernardo from Venezuela, we both did the Librium shuffle to a unit called Tiebout. After another series of tests while still in a Librium daze, I would begin on a new path and interesting journey in the life of Eddie Mackay

Chapter 4 – Hazelden is Discovery –

The initial phase of this strange new journey would last approximately one year. It will always be known to me as *"La-La Land."* I was without a real identity or real thought process. I would continue daily living among many different people, including old friends and acquaintances, acting as if my routines were normal. Honestly, this new experience of abstinence from alcohol sucked. I tried my utmost to make-believe that all was well. The Tiebout unit of Hazelden had been named after Harry Tiebout, the first psychiatrist to give credence to the works of Alcoholics Anonymous. Having later read from the writings of Harry Tiebout, I have no doubt there was no coincidence in my placement in that specific unit. This was one of many such happenings in this interesting path that I have traveled. I do believe, *"There are no coincidences – Just God being anonymous."* I was pretty much resigned to do whatever was being asked of me, to permit my return to continue my work as an engineer. I felt my presence was extremely significant to the ongoing success of Grumman Olson, with any extended absence being problematic. The Hazelden units typically had 21 patients, most of whom would spend 28 days on the unit. One or two patients would arrive daily, while one or two departed. We would meet many different individuals. The unit had three counselors, two assistant counselors, and a Chaplain. A strict housekeeper nicknamed *"Nurse Crotchett"* by some fools, was a very caring woman named Beverly. She was doing a very tough job of maintaining a neat, clean, and orderly facility with 21 alcoholics and addicts, some being quite unpredictable in behavior. I had been assigned to the only female counselor in the unit. She did become quite frustrated on occasion, asking if I would prefer another counselor, but I insisted all was well. The Chaplain was an older gentleman, and we seemed to relate well right from our introduction. Being very much at ease when speaking with him, and he was polite and patient. He did tell me quietly that I lacked honesty about most things we discussed. I did seem to find it easier to become more honest after a couple of sessions. He then challenged me with some seriously written assignments. Those initial assignments being mostly related to the death of my wife Patricia, who had died just four years prior in December 1989. He felt that I had failed to address and process that grief honestly and realistically. This Chaplain had found an area where we could have serious discussions about my whole thinking process, including my increase in consumption of alcohol. That opened one door into the head of this cocky and arrogant Scotsman. Strange to say, I never discussed any of these sessions with my counselor. No doubt, I was becoming much more open and honest in our daily sessions and assignments. Initially, I had been presented with the "Big Book" of Alcoholics Anonymous Third Edition, The Twelve Steps and Twelve Traditions of A.A., and a black book known as Twenty-Four Hours a Day by Hazelden. I have continued to utilize these three books as part of my daily way of living. My "Big Book" has been taped up on many occasions, having traveled many miles. Even although the 4th Edition of this "Big Book" was published in 2001, I felt more at ease with my battered old Third Edition. It was suggested that we all read this ***"Big Book,"*** which I proceeded to do immediately. I read it cover to cover. While being of some interest, it did not seem to apply to me personally. I was now a well-read drunk. Harry Tiebout, in his writings, described the importance of the active alcoholic to reach a personal bottom before having a willingness to make lifestyle changes. Both the Chaplain and my counselor were to use my casual description of the progression of my disease to convince me I had already reached that personal bottom. That off-hand description of my drinking provided in the entry process at Hazelden was well used throughout my stay. In numerous discussions, my own words would come back to haunt me. I had provided an accurate description of the progression of my alcoholism. Becoming somewhat more honest, I knew I had omitted the more serious problems and events that occurred throughout the years. We, alcoholics, have selective memories. We bury so much so easily.

Preserving our ongoing addictive and destructive way of life becomes a real priority. It just seems to happen without any thought or conscious action. The rooms on the Tiebout unit consisted of some four patient rooms, some two patient rooms, and a couple of single bedrooms. Newcomers all started in the four patient rooms. Taking care of bed making and household chores came easy, having spent time on active duty in the U.S. Army. I also lived at home alone after Patricia's death. My housekeeping ability endeared me to Beverly, the Housekeeper. She spent much time teaching grown men how to handle basic housekeeping chores, so I was a favored patient from the beginning. Initially, I was also required to go through a daily physical check-up for that first week. Hazelden had an excellent gymnasium with an indoor track, swimming pool, and all types of physical exercise equipment. The use of this fine facility was encouraged. Due to my excessive weight and high blood pressure, my activities were restricted to walking the track, which I found extremely boring. I chose to walk outdoors around the lake and through the woods in the Minnesota winter weather. Walking whenever I had an opportunity and loving that wooded facility while still in a confused state of mind. My weight of 305 pounds upon arrival was certainly excessive for myself. It now seemed to be of real concern to that doctor at Hazelden, causing my physical activities to be restricted. For most of my adult life, my weight stayed between 160 and 175 pounds. I had been a physically fit individual, and I was now being treated as if my life was in danger. While living in delusion, I successfully ignored any negative health effects of my excessive weight gain over that last ten years. My weight gain was much more significant after my wife Patricia's death in December 1989.

Chapter 5 – Patricia's Death –

Most of my adult life, I had been a very fit and healthy individual. Only visiting doctors when smashing up vehicles or some other destructive act. Required as a corporate officer of Grumman to have an annual physical, that was a dreaded event. Usually receiving comments about my obvious excessive drinking. I would promise to reduce my weight, then proceed with my daily drinking way of life. The increase in my body weight had started in my late forties, causing me to buy new shirts and suits for work. This continued throughout my fifties, with my only concern being the inconvenience of always needing new clothes. My wife Patricia had expressed her worries, and I just blew her off. She wanted me to look my best, and that became a challenge for her.

Along with increased weight had come nosebleeds, both internal and external. The nosebleeds were a source of nuisance and embarrassment, requiring me to carry an ample supply of tissues. Another nuisance item was the swelling of my ankles. This swelling caused real discomfort, with my socks cutting off circulation. This annoying problem was solved by eliminating the wearing socks. I could usually be found wearing an expensive suit, shirt, tie, the best of shoes with no socks. Some of my business associates would kid me about this, but so what. None of these physical problems were any reason to have me quit my daily drinking.

At one period, I had attempted to reduce my daily consumption and refrain from drinking at lunch. I just never went to lunch. It never occurred to me to go for lunch where alcohol wasn't served. My thought process was flawed. While these problems existed before Patricia died, they certainly got much worse afterward.

On that tragic December day of 1989, my loving wife Patricia would pass on so tragically, without any warning, leaving one giant void in my life. I was lost. I had been traveling on a business trip when Patricia's death occurred. My stepdaughter Cathy had made plans to join her mother for their usual Christmas shopping. This would mean Cathy was staying overnight at the farm, while I was off on typical business travels. Just before they would leave home for shopping, my wife Patricia had collapsed. She was rushed to Three Rivers Hospital, where an apparent heart attack was diagnosed. After emergency treatment, she was admitted to a room for further observation.

Cathy had desperately attempted to locate me without any success. I had traveled to Saint Louis to visit with Continental Baking, with an additional planned visit to Frito-Lay in Dallas. Bad weather delayed our flight from Saint Louis to Dallas. No cell phones in those days, so I did not receive the message from Cathy until arrival at the hotel in Dallas. I caught a late flight to Chicago, picked up a rental car, and drove to Three Rivers. Unfortunately, I arrived too late. Patricia had undergone a second heart attack, from which she did not recover. She had already been transferred to the funeral home when I arrived at the hospital. My loving, beautiful, and caring wife had died much too young. I did not handle this loss at all well. Both of my older brothers and my sister came from Vancouver and Edmonton, Canada, to be with me for Patricia`s wake and funeral. We did just what was expected at the wake, with lots of reminiscing, singing, and drinking in excess for three days. It has often been said –*"the only difference between a Scottish wedding and a Scottish funeral was one less drunk at the funeral."* This may have worked well for a temporary fix, but there was now one giant void in my life. As I attempted to return to what I thought was a normal way of daily living, I was one lost individual.

Always being a hard-working individual, I now delved deeper into my engineering work, and my drinking increased. Ten and twelve hours were my typical workdays. Frequently, long airline flights would occur after that long workday. These flights also involved heavy consumption of premium quality Scotch Whisky. It was certainly not unusual to work a full day, and then take a transatlantic flight in first class, grab a rental car, and drive on a strange highway in some other country with a belly full of booze. How I continued to function at such a high level in engineering, while consuming two quarts of Scotch daily, is truly a mystery. My daily life consisted of engineering or traveling, and consumption of Johnnie Walker. I still reflect on that past destructive and delusional lifestyle and marvel that my **"Guardian Angels"** protected me. They worked overtime.

Chapter 6 – The Tiebout Unit –

Being nudged and prodded into this so-called 12 Step process of living while at Hazelden was quite confusing. I had willingly accepted my lack of power over Jonnie Walker Scotch, while not accepting that my life was unmanageable. Having never missed a day of work, even when smashing up vehicles and having a bodily injury, I thought I was managing well. Since I didn't miss work, I didn't have a problem. The reality was I had been managing my alcoholism. That had become a fulltime job. The longer I drank, the more expensive the lawyers became, also appearing less competent. Maintaining my professional appearance as required, along with ongoing management tasks, had been taking much more effort than I had realized. The progression of my disease of chronic alcoholism was quite insidious. Good sense had slipped away, being replaced by delusion. The Tiebout group was in constant flux, with newcomers arriving and old-timers going home or moving on for extended care, so we met a lot of individuals. Group discussions without the counselors were a part of the daily afternoon routine, being interesting and challenging. These informal sessions did seem to work well for me. No doubt that the group could see right through my phony act of superiority. Being the oldest patient chronologically, I was most naive when it came to alcoholism, addiction, and treatment centers. It seemed that everyone else in the group had been exposed to A.A., N.A., or treatment programs before arrival on this unit. I was **"a babe in the woods."** On one afternoon session, it was my turn to be in the center of the group. Doing my best, I was explaining my plans to adopt to 12 Step living after leaving Hazelden, saying just what I thought was expected of me. Still not sold on this abstinence concept, I said that while not intending to drink as I had previously, I may not give up Johnnie Walker entirely. I then stated I wanted to have the ability to control my drinking. I certainly was being serious while trying to be honest. From across the room, a young fellow would ask me – **"Scotsman, don't you want to enjoy your booze?"** I responded with, **"of course,**

I want to enjoy it." He then responded with the statement, *"How can you enjoy it if you have to control it?"* I do believe that was the first light bulb that lit up in the head of this chronic alcoholic. I have never forgotten that moment. I probably owned socks older than this young man, but he was so much smarter when it came to our common problem. Those afternoon sessions on the Tiebout unit of Hazelden introduced me to the concept of *one alcoholic speaking with another alcoholic,* and even more important, *one alcoholic listening to another alcoholic.* This concept of speaking and listening within our fellowship still intrigues me today. I do believe this speaking and listening is a major component of my life in Recovery. A requirement for completion of the Primary Treatment was the completion of Step Five of the twelve steps of A.A. I intended to complete this fifth step and get back to work. I made an effort to understand these steps. Maybe I was treating them as a scholar while feeling they did not apply to me personally. My fifth step was done with the Chaplain. He quite politely told me to go back and start over, explaining that I neither accepted nor understood my problems. Having always been a good scholar in the past, this annoyed me. I then repeated that process doing as directed. Maybe I was beginning to see the light. I tried sincerely with my second session of sharing my fourth step inventory, as required to take my fifth step. He did kindly sign off, just to permit me to have completion. He told me, however, when I found a good sponsor, I would need to repeat this process, with some real emotional honesty. He also emphasized that *"Hazelden was Discovery, and Alcoholics Anonymous was Recovery."* Not having a clue as to what he was trying to tell me, I can still remember it well. He was a patient and caring individual. I was blessed to have met him in those early days when still living in delusion. Progressing along while doing my best to do as directed, I would tell people what I thought they wanted to hear, and life was becoming better. My biggest problem was the lack of sleep. Dreading lying awake and restless night after night. That nice female doctor in Ignatia explained that my system was waking me up demanding alcohol, and the problem would diminish with time. That problem was to continue for approximately two years, although the severity was reduced. When back in my somewhat normal life of **La-La Land,** I still suffered from fatigue due to lack of sleep. Having no problem falling asleep, but shortly after, I would be wide awake, not able to return to sleep. Simply lying wide awake, in my bed at home or in some strange bed on my travels. My head would be going non-stop with so many crazy unrelated thoughts. Later in 1995, when living in Recovery, and having an understanding of the 12 steps process of living, a strange thought occurred. While lying wide awake, I wondered if my inability to have a good night of sleep may not be a mental, physical, or psychological problem, but a character defect. With this new crazy thought in mind, I began to pray at each opportunity to that God of my experience, asking to have that problem removed. Strange as it may seem, it did work for me. While not an instant solution, I was gradually able to get enough real sleep to allow me to function daily without fatigue. I do not question how it works, but gladly accept that it certainly worked to solve my problem. Beginning my fourth week at Hazelden, I was subjected to a meeting with all the counselors, and it seemed they were ganging up on me. They did acknowledge that I was doing everything asked of me, even saying I was having a positive influence on recent newcomers. They felt with the temptations experienced in my engineering life, combined with my long drinking, history that my chances of continued sobriety were minimal at best. They suggested that I should consider an extended stay in the Jellinek unit, followed possibly by some time in the Fellowship Half-Way House. **My immediate response to their idea was *"No Way."*** I explained how much I was missed by my employer, and how many tasks were delayed in my absence. Then proceeding to do my best job of selling them on my understanding of what would be required of me to achieve successful Recovery. Having been privileged to attend two outside A.A. meetings while at Hazelden, I had some limited knowledge of what happened in these meetings. I now proceeded to tell the counselors that I knew how important my attendance and participation in A.A. meetings would be in keeping me sober. ***Plain Mackay Bullshit!*** They cautiously agreed to my release. They would even allow me to depart one day early. This early release had been a special request from Grumman Corporation to permit my deposition to be taken in New Hampshire. This deposition involving Grumman Olson litigation had been delayed due to my being at Hazelden. The counselors would also inform me that being a daily drinker would require I attend daily A.A. meetings. I said that would not be a problem. Being so cocky that I would say, ***"if I drink again, I will get a flight to the Twin Cities, and you can pick me up."*** Saying I would willingly start over, including that extended care idea. I had no idea what I was committing myself to. This rash statement did help me through ***"one more day"*** on a few occasions. There were some evenings on my travels when I did consider some serious drinking, followed by a flight back to Minnesota. Somehow my pride, reluctance to fail and the helping hand of willing members of A.A. got me through one more day of abstinence. I did depart Hazelden to return home on Tuesday, December 7th of 1993, returning to the new world of Eddie Mackay V.P. Engineering of Grumman Olson. I had no idea how I was going to live my life without my daily dose of Johnnie Walker. Foolishly assuming that after my 27 days at Hazelden, I was adequately equipped, I did not have a clue. I did have some reluctant willingness, with an attitude that I could do it. Never being accustomed to failure, I was seriously lacking in humility. No real knowledge of what I might encounter in this new way of life. Many of the members of A.A. would tell me it was just **"One Day at a Time."** This frequently used A.A .quote would cause me to reflect on the quote from Robert Burns, our Ayrshire poet, **"Life is but a Day at Most."** With lots of luck and the blessings of some Higher Power, I would often make it through one more day of abstinence. That quote from Robert Burns surely did help me as I began to travel this new path of life in Recovery.

Chapter 7 – Introduction to Alcoholics Anonymous -

My first challenge was traveling to Boston to meet with a local attorney and Grumman corporate attorney to prepare for a deposition. After some initial discussions in the office of the law firm, we adjourned to a nice restaurant for lunch. A business lunch without a drink was something new and was an unusual experience for me. Both attorneys were aware of my recent visit to Hazelden. They attempted to be supportive by refraining from having a cocktail. Being quite cocky, I assured them that was not a problem. I may have believed it. That first day back to work, I was so Naïve. Our deposition was scheduled for Thursday morning in Bedford, New Hampshire. Driving there easily and returning to Boston, where I got my return flight to Michigan. Boston to Detroit being a typical two drink flight, abstaining on this flight seemed to be no problem. I was aware of my commitment to daily A.A. meetings. Still, I rationalized that would have to begin on Friday, as I arrived home so late on Thursday. Returning to the workplace on Friday was a unique experience. Few people were aware of where I had been, and I had decided now to be quite open and honest about my visit to a treatment center for alcoholism. I was also open about my new anticipated way of life, with my planned involvement in A.A. and abstinence from alcohol. Eddie Mackay was the main topic of the many conversations around engineering and main offices, as well as around the manufacturing facility in Sturgis, Michigan. It did not take long for the word to spread to the other Grumman Olson facilities around the country. My phone just kept ringing, keeping my secretary busy for sure. I had not realized just how well known I was in the aluminum truck body business. That following week consisted of telephone calls from around the United States and Canada, also including a few from Europe, where I had been working with G.M. of Europe, Daimler Benz, and many European bodybuilders. The most surprising calls I received were from engineering and business associates, vendors, and customers who would welcome me into the Fellowship of Alcoholics Anonymous.

People I had known over many years in business, having no idea they were sober alcoholics in Recovery. The many statements of support and encouragement surely felt genuine, and I was quite overwhelmed. As a routine Hazelden procedure, I had been provided with an A.A. contact in Three Rivers, with name, telephone number, and instructions to call. After work on that Friday, I did attempt to contact this individual with no success. Fortunately, an employee at Grumman Olson had come to see me in my office that day, providing a printout of all A.A. meeting locations and times for Saint Joseph County. Having known this individual from the American Legion bar, I had no idea he had quit drinking some years previously. He was quick to extend the hand of A.A to someone in need, with Eddie Mackay being the needy recipient. Quite unaware just how much I needed the help that was now being so willingly offered. Arriving at the Three Rivers A.A. meeting, I met a fellow named Dick S. Conversation revealed that Dick S. lived a little over a mile from my home. He was quick to provide his telephone number, saying to call him anytime. He also provided the latest printed schedule of all A.A .meetings in Saint Joseph and Kalamazoo Counties. Informing me of many more meetings available in Kalamazoo County. Dick S. and I still maintain a friendship in our fellowship of A.A. at the time of this writing. He proved to be extremely helpful in those early days of abstinence. On Wednesday of the following week, I arrived early at the A.A. meeting in Sturgis, the city where I worked. As I looked across the room, my eyes connected with a young man named Rick M. Having known Rick for many years as a crazy, wild, hard-drinking young man, this was a surprise. The last time our paths had crossed was at the courthouse, where we were both paying fines for alcohol-related offenses. Leaving the courthouse, we had both gone across the street to the bar. I had known Rick as a high school student when I advertised in the local paper looking for someone to shear my seven sheep. Rick answered my ad. I also knew his family of drinkers and card players. Frequently drinking with his father in the local bar. I now discovered that Rick had already been involved in A.A. for over six months. We both continue our special friendship today. While our initial friendship was in A.A., that was later expanded into my farming life, with my involvement in Highland Cattle. We have both been blessed with having quite a unique relationship and an extraordinary way of life. Two recovered alcoholic livestock farmers in a serious partnership that has developed over 26 years. December 1993 and January 1994, this new way of life and work, including A.A. meetings and abstinence, was strange. I doubt that I could ever provide an accurate description of those weird days and sleepless nights. Having spent a lifetime of subconsciously aiming to impress people, I was now acting as if all was well with this new sober lifestyle. When asked by my cohorts how I was doing? I would quickly respond, **"Fine."** Later a good friend explained to me the real meaning of **FINE** was *"F—cked up, Insecure, Neurotic, and Emotional."* I was going through the motions at work, but my head was not functioning in a normal manner. I could not think straight. I was confused. Foolishly still dumb enough to continue having lunch with my old drinking lunch-time buddies, and not drink. I would tell them everything was great. ***Not too smart!*** I did make daily A.A. meetings between Three Rivers, Sturgis, Marcellus Vicksburg, and Centreville. My biggest problem was the lack of sleep. I could go to sleep easily, then be wide awake after two hours, and that was it. Fatigue was a problem, along with the daily challenges of truck body engineering. I was extremely stressed and did not want to talk about it. Acting as if all was normal while not knowing if I was afoot or on horseback. As a condition of my release from Hazelden, I had agreed to commence with weekly counseling. The counselor was in Kalamazoo, but made weekly visits to Sturgis, so a meeting was scheduled. The first meeting was canceled due to the weather. The second due to my being out of town, and then came the holiday season. I eventually met with this counselor in early January of 1994. She possessed my file furnished by Hazelden. Not sure what that file contained, but it seemed she had already formed an opinion of Eddie Mackay before our meeting. Our initial questions and answers did not go so well. She seemed sure I would relapse. since I had previously enjoyed a good life while drinking heavily. I was quick to ask her if she was a clean addict or a sober drunk? She responded that she had never had any problems with addiction and never would have. This prompted me to request that my session the following week would involve a different counselor. Explaining that we were advised while at Hazelden that we should only counsel for addiction with someone who had walked in our moccasins. Taking offense, she informed me that changing counselors was not an option. Stating that I would be required to complete the series of sessions with her as my counselor. My response was **"No Way,"** and our brief session was over. Later that week, I would receive a telephone call from the counseling service in Kalamazoo, informing me that changing my counselor was not an option. Ending these sessions did not bother me at all. Soon to discover that I would be required to pay for this service out of my pocket was annoying. My health insurer declined coverage of the expenses since I had failed to fulfill the total requirement. The costs levied for this complete program seemed to be outrageous. Eventually being reduced in negotiation, but still costly. I would rationalize that I had often spent much more on lawyers who were not much better than this counselor had been. January 1994 had brought a new year with a completely different way of life. I was now attempting to continue working as an engineer without my normal daily dose of alcohol. I have heard this described as ***"white-knuckling it."*** It was strange, I was confused, and it sucked

Chapter 8 – Traveling in Early Recovery-

Never having been able to describe what these early days and weeks of abstinence were like, but abstinence sucks. I would later accept that they were a necessity along my path to sobriety. I am convinced that ***"God has a strange sense of humor."*** Early February of 1994 had me back on the road again, scheduled to take the evening flight from Chicago`s O`Hare to Frankfurt, Germany. Company policy stated we should fly Business Class. American Airlines was good at providing regulars with seats in First Class if space was available. There was always space on that evening flight that I had taken so often. My thoughts that evening as I waited to board was, how much Perrier could I drink on that long flight? As usual in First Class, the Stewardess would serve drinks before departure.

Having taken this flight previously, the Stewardess remembered me well, asking if I would have my usual Johnnie Walker? I stuttered and said I would be traveling without alcohol. Then explaining that I had been to Hazelden for treatment. She smiled, saying, "that is great, and I hope you get involved in A.A. they have done wonders with my uncles, and we would wish for my father to try it, but he is too stubborn." This extremely nice Stewardess talked to me most of the way to Germany. I never considered taking a drink—another miracle along my path. I had no trouble with my daily task of finding the English Speaking A.A. meetings, being quite surprised at the large turnout. Many of the members were using English as their second language, being Europeans who did not understand the local dialect. With the Berlin Wall going down in 1989 and the new European Union being formed, so many companies were setting up new facilities throughout Europe.

Many of these A.A .members were businessmen on travel. Many had long-term sobriety. While I was still just going through the motions and not yet being a real believer in 12 Step Recovery, I would say what I thought they would like to hear. Much too proud to reach out for help. I was usually the newcomer, and others would reach out to me. The meetings after the meetings were always a lifesaver in those early days of travel. We would often speak of everything other than Recovery. I felt quite comfortable with this unique fellowship. Life during the routine workday was no problem. At the end of the day, it was tough. When my associates were heading to a restaurant where they might eat but always drank, leaving them was difficult. I was heading to the hotel to clean up and find the A.A. meeting. It was not easy, but after that meeting and the typical follow-up meeting, I was usually all set, having survived one more day of abstinence. On a few occasions, I did consider just getting right with it and drink with my friends. My pride, stubborn nature, and ego would get me past those thoughts. As I reflect now, it was my character defects that often saved me from myself. What I thought of as strengths would later be recognized as shortcomings. My routine when traveling in Europe involved a detour through Scotland on my return flight to the U.S. Just for a short visit, which usually involving drinking in the Scottish pubs. Now, these visits meant attending the Scottish A.A. meetings. I would often participate in two meetings a day in Scotland, and they were great meetings. They were 90 minute-meetings instead of one-hour meetings in the U.S. Always the meetings after the meetings, which helped me a lot. Somehow these Scottish meetings enabled me to really buy-in more to the Fellowship of Alcoholics Anonymous.

I recall, on one occasion, when sharing at a meeting in Glasgow, I said I intended to give A.A. a chance. From across the table, a real Glaswegian responded, stating, *"A.A. is doing quite well with or without you, Eddie, and doesn`t need a chance. Why don`t you get your shite together and give yourself a chance."* I was humbled indeed. I needed to be put straight. I would accept it from that blunt Scotsman. I still continue to have a daily need to find more humility. With my ego also requiring deflation as I travel along this path of Recovery. I think Eddie`s Ego could be deflated today and then be riding horseback tomorrow. *- Progress, not Perfection.*

Chapter 9 - My First Tiebout Reunion -

March of 1994 found me back at Hazelden for the annual Tiebout Reunion from Thursday (Saint Patrick`s Day) through Sunday. I will remember that occasion quite well. I had received notices of the upcoming reunion, which were ignored, as I white-knuckled those early days of abstinence. Arriving home from an A.A. meeting in Vicksburg one evening, I heard my phone ringing. I was barely able to answer it, and I had no answering machine in those days. A nice woman from Hazelden said that they had not yet received my reservation for the Tiebout Reunion, and she was sure I would want to attend. I found myself saying, *"sure - I will be there,"* and I don't know who's voice answered, as I had never considered attending that event. I did make the room reservation while on the telephone, and the next day proceeded to make an airline reservation for the flight from Kalamazoo to Minneapolis/Saint Paul. I do not have a clue as to why I had responded that way. I got that usual 7.00 am flight from Kalamazoo, being picked up by the driver on arrival at the Minneapolis airport. Once more, we made that trip to Center City and Hazelden. This time I was checked into the Renewal Center as opposed to the Ignatia unit. Receiving a warm welcome as the only newcomer for that special event. There were 62 attendees at that reunion, and the strong fellowship within that group amazed me. The obvious superstar of that fine group had arrived, and everyone was out front to welcome him. This was the renowned George Weller, being unloaded from an old beat-up Dodge van, along with a huge powered-wheelchair. George was an easy 350 pounds, and while he could walk around alright, he needed the wheelchair to travel any real distance. He also used oxygen and had his bottle hanging from a strap. It seemed he had emphysema, and on occasions, needed the oxygen. He was a huge and loud man in his late sixties, who wheezed when he laughed, and he laughed a lot. George was the head counselor of the Tiebout unit for many years, having retired before my arrival there in 1993. I heard his name frequently, as it was said that I should have been there earlier since I was an obvious candidate for counseling by Weller. I had no idea what they were speaking about or why they thought I needed Weller. It seemed that George had been the expert in ego deflation. They thought I had an inflated ego, along with arrogance and lack of humility. I introduced myself to this famous George Weller. He asked a few questions and said, *" well, I was nearly as old as you when I got sober, so if you join this bunch here, you do have a chance,"* and off he went to speak with other members. The second

"Superstar" to show up was a very tall senior citizen by the name of Paul H. Paul lived nearby in Wisconsin and was an active participant at all Renewal Center events. He had a long, eventful history with Hazelden. Both George Weller and Paul H. would be significant in my progress in Recovery. I am forever indebted to their suggestions, encouragement, and their *"cut out the bullshit attitude"* with me. Many of the attendees were from the Twin Cities and neighboring Wisconsin. There were also attendees from across the United States and Hawaii, with one also from Sweden. There was lots of sobriety, with myself being the only newcomer. The next four days they kept me busy. Although well treated, I did not quite feel I was one of the group. Maybe just my perception. I did have the good fortune to have breakfast and spend time alone with George Weller. We spoke about my efforts and struggles with the fourth Step issues. Lots of talk in the A.A. fourth step is about our fears. I was quick to state that I was fearless, and fear was of no concern. George sat back and said, *"when you wake up and find the fear that kept you out there so long, you might stand a chance."* Challenging me always gets some action. Later with deep digging, I was to uncover that fear that George had referenced. My deep-rooted fear that kept me going was the *fear to depart the familiar*. No matter how bad the situation is, we feel sure we can handle what is familiar. When meeting with George a year later, we did delve into my buried fears and worked on my flawed thinking. He spoke a lot on that subject of fear, also telling me that **FEAR,** when active, meant *"F—ck everything and run."* In Recovery, **FEAR** meant, *"Face everything and recover."* He had lots of gems for the newcomer. He would also point out that sobriety was for grown-ups. We, active alcoholics, are childlike in so many ways. We want what we want, and we want it now. Usually, we want what is yours also. Not easy to begin growing up at 58 years old. Departure was after lunch on Sunday when I was offered a ride back to the airport instead of using the Hazelden driver. George Weller was being picked up by his wife and son with the same old Dodge van. While his son was loading the huge wheelchair in the back using a plywood ramp, I asked George why he did not have a van equipped with a wheelchair lift? His response was *"tough enough just to afford this old van on social security, never mind a fancy van with a lift."* I mentally took some notes of the year and model of his Dodge van, as a crazy thought had entered my head. One of my many projects at Grumman Olson involved designing buses with provisions for wheelchair lifts. Although we did not manufacture the wheelchair lifts or ramps, we produced buses, ambulances, and rescue vehicles with provisions for their installation. I was familiar with many unique designs of lifts and ramps. I suggested to George that I could make him a lift to help load his wheelchair into the back of his old van. In his gruff way, he said he did not want anything to block the rear windows of the van. He then departed, but my head was already in gear. As everyone was departing and saying their farewells, there were lots of talking about seeing you next year. I was echoing the group and promising to return for the 1995 Tiebout Reunion. Paul H. had his arm around my shoulder. He quietly stated, *"Eddie, alcoholics are great at making promises, but we who are sober do keep them."* I am sure that was meant as a challenge that I would accept, saying once more, *"I will be here in 1995."* I am so glad that I was challenged that day, as I did return in 1995. Also, returning each year for the Tiebout Reunion through March of 2019. Recent reunions identify me as the senior citizen of the reunion group, and I do my utmost to continue the great traditions. No one can ever replace George Weller or Paul H. at such events. Many of those *Wellerism's* are now known as *Mackayism's*. Upon arrival at the Renewal Center each year, I will always look at the photo of Paul H. in the display case. It provides that feeling of being blessed by meeting him. I can always recall Paul saying the only things needed to get me started was, *"Don't Drink – Turn my life over to the Care of God - Get rid of all of my old ideas."* I do feel blessed to be inspired by his simplistic way of thinking. At some reunions, I have been honored to be an evening speaker. Quite an experience to be standing in that Bigelow Auditorium, looking over the many faces, knowing I was one such person in 1993. I am able and willing to accept without any reservation *the miracle of Recovery!* I believe the Tiebout alumni and George Weller initiated the first reunion with the completion of the Renewal Center. That original group contained members of Tiebout that I met in 1994. At one reunion, we created a listing of attendees with e-mail addresses. One member also created a Tiebout webpage to permit continued internet communication. Hazelden being initially reluctant to endorse this effort due to maintaining strict anonymity. Our group updated our e-mail listing at each reunion. Many of us would maintain contact throughout the year. Today the internet is an accepted tool in ongoing communications in recovery groups. I continue to receive **Today`s Gift** by e-mail from Hazelden each morning. This e-mail is then forwarded to many others with my comments added. Just part of a daily routine that works so well for me. Hopefully, it has also been helpful to many others. Reflecting on the impact of the reunions on my Recovery, I feel that I *came* to Hazelden for treatment. Then I *came to* during the early A.A. meetings. Finally, I *came to believe* after attending my first reunion.

This is where I was convinced of the miracle of Recovery, and a new way of life had begun, even although I still had lots of skepticism and doubts.

Chapter 10 – Finding Sobriety -

Returning to a busy work schedule, I was struggling. living alone, and maintaining the farm with a few sheep, while continuing daily A.A. meetings, including abstinence from alcohol, was not an easy way of life. I was faking it the best I could. Life was not all bad, but it was different. While there was an improvement, I was not sure who I was, and not sure I liked whoever I was trying to be. I was no doubt in *La-La Land.* Even with my busy work schedule, I found time to develop a unique all-aluminum loading ramp to facilitate the loading of George Weller`s oversized wheelchair. This was a unique loading ramp. It would fold up into the rear of the van, then swivel for storage on the left rear side to leave the rear windows clear. I had been able to find an identical Dodge van to the one George had in a used car lot. Borrowing that van provided assurance, this ramp would work as anticipated. Calling George Weller, I was directed to ship the ramp to a body repair shop in Minneapolis. I never received any response as to how this ramp worked, or if it was satisfactory. My life in engineering in 1994 was hectic, with my head in confusion. With lots of travel to Canada, Europe, Mexico, Brazil, and Venezuela. I would never miss that daily A.A. meeting. English speaking meetings were always available, no matter where I traveled. I am not sure that I was a believer in this Twelve Steps Way of Life, but determined to make a real effort. I certainly received plenty of support and encouragement on my travels and at home in Michigan. I am not sure how I survived those days of abstinence, with the sleepless nights and the resulting fatigue. Someone was always there at the right time and right place to keep me on the right path. I was convinced to sign up for a **"Big Book Workshop"** in October 1994. It would consist of four sessions. Friday evening, Saturday forenoon, Saturday afternoon, and Sunday forenoon. Being organized by the A.A. groups from Battle Creek, Michigan, they had come around our local A.A. meetings, since they needed fifty participants to cover the costs. I signed up, being the only member from Three Rivers, but four members I knew from Sturgis had also signed up for the event. The format of this workshop was a take-off of the **"*Joe and Charlie routine.*"** These two renowned A.A. members from Little Rock, Arkansas, had created a routine. They traveled to many locations providing their interpretation of the 12 steps process of living. They had also included some humor in the process, and I am a great believer in using humor today. That humor may often be a wee bit sick and not make sense to *"Normies."* If we alcoholics cannot laugh at our previous lives, we will miss the joke of the century. I was not smiling much in those early days of **La-La Land,** but I love to smile today, often causing people to wonder what I am smiling about. The location for this workshop event was at a bar with a restaurant on Highway 66 just north of Athens, Michigan. This bar also happened to be a watering hole that I frequented when driving from Detroit to Sturgis. It was a typical noisy bar with a dartboard and pool table and had private dining rooms at the rear available to rent. We were required to walk through the common bar area to get to the room for the workshop on a busy Friday evening. The two individuals who had been brought in to put on this event were Mark from Texas and Joe from California, with both having significant years in Recovery. One of them was originally from Battle Creek. They were one of many such teams that do these events around the United States. Doing it for free, and only expecting their airline fares and hotel accommodations would be reimbursed. They began with the first page of the Third Edition of the book of Alcoholics Anonymous, ending the fourth session at Sunday lunch with Page 164 of that book. Typically, one of them would go through a portion of the book, then we would have questions, answers, and discussion. Then the other one would take over, repeating that process. Friday evening went well, and Saturday morning with lunch served to the group before an afternoon session. On arrival Sunday morning, we had a problem finding someone to open the bar. Then getting past the bar to the private room was challenging, with the stink of old stale beer and urine, as the bar had closed late with no clean up performed. Not a first-time experience for most of us, but certainly the first time in abstinence for myself. The smell would have gagged a maggot. Quite the location to convene this A.A. workshop! Maybe I had been to enough meetings and heard enough members sharing, and probably because Mark and Joe were so good. My mind was now opened to look and read this book in a completely different manner. I started all over as had been suggested, inserting *"Eddie"* into many of the stories. This was the beginning of a personal fascination with this book known as *"The Big Book"* by many. I am convinced that the original writers were God Inspired. A few weeks later was Thanksgiving, and I headed to an early morning A.A.

meeting in Kalamazoo. I planned to stay home, relax, and watch football games. As that day progressed, I would reflect on how miserable I had been on the previous Thanksgiving. I had been sitting in Hazelden, detoxed, confused, and trying to accept how I ever I got there. I could not think straight, I could not sleep, and I could not concentrate on watching the football game on television. I was miserable. Now within a year, I could seriously look at what was happening in my life. I felt sure I was on the right path. Also, realizing I may have to change just about everything of that old life to continue this new way of living. I realized this new way of living and thinking was not all about *not drinking,* even if that was a necessity. I told myself *I could do it. I would do it. I would not fail.* I also considered that part of that change in lifestyle may require giving up my career as V.P. of Engineering to concentrate on fixing up my old farm. Possibly I could find work as an engineer somewhere that did not involve traveling. Fixing the old farm had been my goal when I purchased the neglected apple farm in 1977. I had certainly done some fixing in the eighties, when I worked at those many tasks on weekends, while still managing to drink enough. After my wife Patricia had died so suddenly in December of 1989, it seemed I was no longer motivated. While I still talked about fixing, I would spend my time drinking and putting off the tasks until the next weekend.- *Procrastination*.

Now with the discovery at Hazelden, daily participation in the meetings of Alcoholics Anonymous, abstinence, and support from the fellowship, this new life of Recovery was just beginning. Being exposed to so many helpful members in my extensive travels had opened my mind. Blessed on many occasions to survive one more day of abstinence, thanks to the hand of A.A. always being there. Culminating with that unique *Big Book Workshop,* I had changed. Starting along this new path, I had a new attitude towards life. Knowing I had indeed experienced many unexplained blessings. My skepticism and cynicism had just slipped away. Being willing to accept that I needed to make that decision to recover, and be willing to go to any lengths to get sober was a big step. I would quit studying and analyzing and start doing what was being suggested by the helpful mentors. *I would find sobriety.* Difficult to define, but I had experienced something entirely different, sitting alone on that Thanksgiving-day of 1994. I had found humility. My attitude towards God had changed. I had become another person with a new way of thinking. ***Discovery would now lead to Recovery.***

Meeting Rooms of Alcoholics Anonymous in Glasgow, Scotland

Meeting Location of Alcoholics Anonymous in Mexico City

Chapter 11 – Changing Vocation -

During 1994 many aerospace and defense contractors had been merging. Grumman Aerospace and Martin Marietta seemed likely candidates for a friendly merger. Suddenly Northrup Corporation made an unfriendly move to take over Grumman, causing increased Grumman Stock prices. Suited me as I had some stock options. Grumman had previously started the process of selling off its various commercial subsidiaries, with Grumman Olson being the largest. When speaking to some friends at Grumman Corporation about possibly giving up my engineering career, I was informed to not even consider such action. It seemed that Eddie Mackay was considered a valued asset of the truck body division, and the sale of Grumman Olson was close to finalization. Northrop Corporation did finally become successful in that unfriendly takeover of Grumman Corporation, with the potential sale of the truck company being placed on hold. This prompted my submission of an application for an amenable severance from Grumman. This was a nice program Grumman had initiated to prevent the sudden loss of key employees. This severance package consisted of a week of salary for each year of service. The company could then determine the exact date of termination, within one year of employee submission. Being classified as a key employee with 34 years of service, it seemed like a good idea. A lot of turmoil within the truck company and within my head. When my two good friends at corporate headquarters responsible for my visit to Hazelden heard of this decision, they did everything possible to change my mind. Telling me that major decisions like this were to be avoided in early sobriety. I responded that it would be no problem, as I was doing fine. Maybe I even believed it. Their genuine concern did scare me some, although I would not admit it. I now knew that my life would change significantly within the next year. After the takeover of Grumman by Northrop Corporation, it was decided to cancel that pending sale of the truck body division. A new management team from the Vought Aircraft Division of Northrop arrived to manage the Grumman Olson and Long-Life Vehicle divisions. The LLV division was producing the U.S. Post Office vehicles at a rate of 100 units per day and very profitable. We had separated this division from the normal Grumman Olson trucks for accounting purposes. I did my best in educating this new management team on the intricacies of this very specialized aluminum truck body business, which we dominated in the United States and Canada. We were truly a niche business in the automotive industry. We produced the aluminum bodies for mounting and integrating with chassis manufactured by all major automotive manufacturers. This necessitated extremely close engineering relationships with these manufacturers. Integrating seating, driver restraints, systems, and controls required for a completed vehicle required special skills. Communication was critical to guarantee compliance with all Federal Motor Vehicle Safety Standards. We were a very specialized producer in the large automotive industry. Eddie Mackay`s engineering team was considered highly qualified in this unique niche business. I was also active in the Society of Automotive Engineers, I maintained close relationships with most members of The American Aluminum Association. Providing insight into our niche business was certainly not an easy task with this new management team. I was willing to share my experience and expertise. All of the developing projects, including a partnership with G.M. of Europe and Latin America, had all been canceled. Traveling would be reduced, which suited me. Maybe my arrogance and ego were not helpful with this difficult task of educating this new management team. Attempting to explain our unique position in the large automotive business seemed futile. So much of our ongoing business was extremely dependent on close relationships with the engineering, marketing, and financial departments of the chassis manufacturers, like General Motors, Ford, Dodge, Navistar, Isuzu, and Daimler Benz. These relationships had been established with many varied individuals over time, as we worked together to satisfy the needs of common customers. This new team had an attitude of **"we will show the yokels how to run a business."** Northrop was obligated to honor my amenable severance, taking effect by October 1995. I was still somewhat surprised when being notified that I would be terminated effective March 31st of 1995. Having suspected my departure was imminent, with diplomacy not being my greatest attribute, it was still unexpected. I had started preparing for my new life as a farmer, but it was still a wee bit scary to make the change. Part of my severance included my being available as a consultant for one year. For my monthly paycheck, I was expected to provide a nominal number of hours. Additional hours would be at an agreed consultant fee rate. I was also expected to be available as required as a consultant for any litigation involving Grumman Olson. It was not easy walking away from that truck body engineering life. That life had consumed my whole being for so many years. I was nervous about how I would handle this new vocation. Also, having a good feeling that it was best for my peace of mind. I received many offers of support and encouragement from many friends in the recovery community.

Retirement was a Misnoma—Actually a Change in Vocation

Chapter 12 – Living in Sobriety -

Between Thanksgiving of 1994 and March 31st of 1995, my whole attitude towards this new way of life in sobriety had a new meaning. Although nervous about giving up engineering and going farming, I felt sure I could manage the change. Financially I would have no immediate problems since I would be receiving my normal salary for 34 weeks plus consulting fees. My whole attitude towards the 12 Step process of living had certainly changed. I had worked through these steps with lots of help and suggestions from the many people met at the many different meetings I attended. Eddie Mackay, the engineer in early sobriety, was becoming a different person with a different way of thinking. I was beginning to find some serenity and peace of mind. George Weller had informed me that if I stuck with Alcoholics Anonymous, I would find **serendipity**. His definition of serendipity was *"like looking for a needle in the haystack and finding the farmer's daughter."* I liked that definition. I believe that during that year in **La-La Land,** while not drinking, I had a feeling of deprivation. I was depriving myself on a daily and sometimes hourly basis, from drinking the Johnnie Walker that I was sure I wanted and needed, just to be myself. After that spiritual awakening or whatever we may call it, on Thanksgiving 1994, I would understand that I was being blessed each day to not need that drink for that given day. Even if I still thought I wanted it, and even if I thought I needed it, and although I knew it would taste good and feel good, I just did not need it. I had come to understand there is a difference between wants and needs. I accepted that I could not continue meeting with the fellows from my drinking days. Unless they were willing to come and visit me on the farm where I could be comfortable being abstinent. One of my old drinking friends asked me one day if I ever felt like going to the local bar? My quick response was, *"when Daniel got out of the Lion's Den, he did not go back for his hat."* Many of those old drinking buddies drifted away, while a few friends still dropped in to visit. If they were drinking a beer, it did not bother me at all. I still did need to avoid the bars. Much later, I found I could even stop into a drinking place, providing I had a real purpose for being there, other than drinking. I could even keep cold beer in my refrigerator for my hillbilly friend, who continued to help me with my farm fixing tasks. The alcohol was not my problem. It was the *"ism."* George Weller had explained that meant *I, Self, and Me*. George had convinced me that, *"I am the problem – We are the solution."* Returning to the 1995 Reunion, I had arrived early at the Renewal Center. I anxiously awaited the arrival of the great George Weller. As was usual, there were many people outside in a nasty Minnesota March day welcoming George, and I was included. While his son was unloading the wheelchair, I observed him using that special aluminum loading ramp. Then George looked around until he found me. He grabbed me and hugged me, squeezing the air out of my lungs, hollering loudly as George, and saying, *"I have met a lot of new drunks, but this Scotsman is special, he keeps his word, and he is one smart guy."* I was now special to George Weller due to making a *"Mackay Ramp"* that made it easier to load his wheelchair. He would repay me ten-fold. That story was talked about so much that I was truly embarrassed. During that Reunion in March of 1995, I would spend as much time with George Weller and Paul H. as possible. They were both quick to send me to read and digest different parts of our so-called *"Big Book."* I may still have been reading it too much as a scholar, and not enough as a chronic alcoholic in recovery, but I had made progress. Paul H. would provide real encouragement by telling me I was on the right path. He said all I had to do was stick with the winners. Having strived to be a winner my whole life, that was a suggestion I would gladly accept. Paul H. also told me the only way to make sense out of change was to plunge into it, move with it, and join the dance. I was now aware that I had become two separate people, as my alcoholism had progressed. I was not sure I had liked either one of those two people. Now I was still not yet sure who I was but felt I knew who I did not want to be. My involvement in A.A .was giving me a new process of thinking. I was moving in the right direction. I was developing some real willingness, with much more open-mindedness, and eventually, I would find emotional honesty. I had also developed some daily disciplined routines to help keep me on the right track. I found that I needed those daily routines, and I had developed an attitude of gratitude. I was not as good as I wanted to be, but certainly better than I used to be! When reading the story of Doctor Bob, co-founder of Alcoholics Anonymous, I would recognize a similarity. I accepted, just like

Doctor Bob, that my consumption of alcohol was a privilege that I had abused. Therefore I no longer had that privilege. I was accepting some responsibility for my alcoholism. This helped in removing that feeling of deprivation. That had caused so much grief and frustration at the beginning of my journey. I would accept the *"Big Book"* statement on Page 58 - *"Remember that we deal with alcohol-cunning, baffling, powerful."* I could also add *"patient"* to the list. It was told to me that my disease was out in the parking lot, doing one-armed pushups awaiting an opportunity. Daily maintenance of a fit spiritual condition had to become a routine, with no exception or excuse. I am only required to be aware of my disease *"Upon Awakening – Throughout the Day – and When I retire at Night."* The rest of the time, I can ignore it. Sometimes I believe that my serenity comes more from what I overlook than from what I might do. I think I am more interested in what will bring me peace than what may provide me with pleasure. As I reflect, I think my successes with the many compliments had added to my delusion. Now I am more interested in what I might add to a balanced way of life. While A.A. had not opened the door to heaven, it had slammed the door on the Hell of my previous destructive life.

Hazelden is Discovery—Alcoholics Anonymous is Recovery

Chapter 13 – Service in Alcoholics Anonymous -

Friday evening of my last day of employment at Northrup Grumman found me at my daily A.A. meeting. A member friend was aware of my new status and asked me if I would be able to give him a ride to the A.A. meeting at the county jail on Tuesday at 10 am. He participated in these weekly jail meetings along with two other longtime A.A members who were "Michigan Snowbirds" that had not returned from Florida and Arizona. He had been doing his utmost to keep the meetings going. His driving license was revoked due to numerous violations. He was soliciting assistance with transportation to the jail each week from other members of the A.A. group. I agreed to pick him up in Three Rivers, where he managed a grocery store, to take him to Saint Joseph County Jail in Centreville on Tuesday, April 5th of 1995. Never had I considered that I might enter that facility voluntarily. This A.A. meeting in the classroom of the jail was quite an experience. It seemed that I knew many of the inmates attending this meeting from my drinking days. Most being surprised to find me in this meeting, not being aware I had stopped drinking. I had been well known as a hard drinker all around the area, and now here I was in an A.A.. jail meeting. I continued to provide transportation each Tuesday morning until my friend had his license reinstated. I continue to carry on these same jail meetings for these many years that I have been blessed with sobriety. Tuesday at 10.00 am, I head to the county jail, where I can meet my replacement while carrying a message of hope to those willing to participate in the A.A. Twelve-Step meeting. That friend that introduced me to jail meetings left the area in 1996. I was asked to consider taking his place on the Saint Joseph County Community Corrections Advisory Board. While A.A traditions prevent anyone from representing A.A on such an advisory board, he had been representing Recovery as an individual, being elected as the "Citizen at Large' member. I did agree that I would give this a try, and have continued to be re-elected, still enjoying being an active participant at the monthly meetings after so many years. Hopefully, I have been able to represent the recovery community in some positive way. One of my goals has been to put a positive face on recovery. When mentioning the word alcoholic or addict to the *"Normies,"* they usually have a mental image that is always negative. When using the term *"Recovered Alcoholic or Addict,"* they will draw a blank. It has been said that describing recovery to a *Normie* is like describing an organism to a *Eunuch.* The members I have met on this board are aware that recovery is quite possible, and also quite probable with our twelve steps way of living. I try to convince them that most of us alcoholics are not bad people needing to get good, but sick people that need to get well. This board has been instrumental in having the county add a Sobriety Court, Drug Court, and Swift and Sure program as alternatives to jail and prison for addicts and alcoholics. I chose to break my anonymity while being respectful to the anonymity of the many members of A.A. and N.A. In this local community, I am as anonymous as a Barber Shop Pole. It has been said that Faith, Fellowship, and Service will cure the World's Ills.

Saint Joseph County Courthouse—Centreville Michigan

Chapter 14 – Becoming a Livestock Farmer -

That spring of 1995 found me accepting the challenge of fixing up the farm. When purchasing the farm in 1977, our initial efforts had been mainly to make the old house habitable. We had accomplished that task with my wife Patricia, being the driving force. In the eighties, I had installed new perimeter fencing while also fixing the old barn and garage buildings. Just reinforcing and re-siding the old buildings provided adequate space for my few sheep and hay storage. Purchasing an old Farmall tractor and bush hog mower, I had proceeded to chop the weeds and brush that covered most of the open ground. The Prairie River ran through the southern portion of the acreage that was flood-plain, swampy, and overgrown with high weeds and brush. This property had been an original forty acres homestead, with the house built in 1871. I had purchased the old farmhouse and buildings with 34 acres. An acre plot in the northeast and five acres on the west side had been sold previously. It had been a productive apple farm, prior to many years of neglect. There still existed 78 apple trees of various types that had been neglected. Having had only a few sheep, I now had plans to increase the size of the flock. Also, deciding to find some Scottish Highland Cattle to graze the property and provide some freezer beef. Raised in Scotland and spending much of my time on a dairy farm in Ayrshire, the farming life was in my blood. Having no prior experience with beef cattle, I had good overall knowledge of working with dairy cattle. I researched where to find some Highland cows and purchased five heifers from a farm in Warsaw, Indiana. Turning them loose, they headed for the swamp and brush areas near the river, and I was lucky to ever find them as they roamed the weed-covered overgrown area. Those busy days of physical work outdoors on the farm in my early sobriety were a real blessing—a radical change for sure, with a different way of thinking. My physical health being steadily improved with all of my daily activities. I would never miss my regular meeting of Alcoholics Anonymous. This daily routine of outdoor farming life seemed right for me.

Scottish Highland Cattle may be as addictive as Johnnie Walker
Livestock Farming in Sobriety—A Spiritual Way of Life

A New Vocation – Or just returning to a Previous Way of Life

Chapter 15 – My Young Life and Scottish Heritage–

Getting involved in farming chores took me back to my boyhood years on the dairy farm. I was born in Kilmarnock, Scotland, at an early age, the youngest of my mother's four kids in four years. My birthdate was February 29th 1936, so maybe I was a wee bit odd from the beginning. My father, also named Eddie Mackay, was employed as a clerk with the London Midland and Scottish Railroad. He was exceptionally good with numbers. On payday, some of his drinking friends would bet on his ability to count faster than any other clerk using the newest adding machines of those times. My father could add four columns of numbers simultaneously. Eddie Mackay never lost, and they would all head to the local pub and drink until closing time. He was an abusive drunk, known to beat on my mother when drunk. Serious stomach ulcer problems and major surgery caused him to quit drinking, and he lived until 75 years of age. The Mackay's were long-time residents of the Strathnaver region of the Scottish Highlands. My grandfather came south by way of Dunfermline to Glasgow, where my father was born. My father spent much of his young adult life in the British Army, maintaining a very military-like stature with his disciplined attitude. His presence seeming larger than his small physical body would indicate. My mother, Gertie Black, a precocious young girl of sixteen when meeting my father in the workplace. She soon became pregnant with my oldest brother Garry. As was typical in those times, this resulted in their marriage, with my father being twelve years older than my mother. Three more kids would follow in four years, making life difficult for this young teenage mother. In September 1939, Great Britain declared war on Germany after the invasion of Poland. The German troops then pushed right across Europe, only to be stalled at the French coast by the English Channel. Great Britain now proceeded to enlist everyone available into military service. That would include my father, even with his advanced age and previous military service. Off to war, he went. My mother was required to take employment in the shipyard in Troon. My two brothers and sister were shipped off to Glasgow into the care of my paternal grandparents. My mother and myself were relocated from Kilmarnock to the village of Dundonald to live with my maternal grandmother Lizzie Black, and my cousin Winnie Black. Winnie was the illegitimate daughter of my mother's older sister, who had been shipped off to America after giving birth. My grandmother would raise Winnie as her daughter. Typical of those times. Winnie and I became close in my younger years. She acted very much like an older sister. She was drafted into the Women's Land Army, working in a local nursery that grew much-needed vegetables and fruits. Many of the women from the Land Army worked on the farms, with most young men being enlisted into the armed forces. Maybe one good thing about the war was that it was a great equalizer. The severe rationing applied to rich and poor, with everyone required to join in the common defense against the powerful Nazi Regime. Before America entered the war, the collapse of Great Britain seemed imminent. An exciting time to grow up, and I doubt as kids, we comprehended just how desperate the situation was. It was exciting for me as an impressionable youngster. We had military bases all around us, with a big army camp, navy base, local air force unit with temporary runways created with steel matting over farm fields, and the U.S. air force based at Prestwick aerodrome. Our Dundonald village was only ten miles from where Nazi cabinet member Rudolph Hess made his parachute landing near Fenwick. He had flown a Messerschmitt 110 from Germany, avoiding the British defense system. Quite an achievement considering the barrage balloons around the area of the Clyde Shipyards. He made a low altitude parachute jump and landed in the Eaglesham moor near Fenwick. He was quickly taken prisoner by the local Home Guard. The mystery of what news he allegedly brought from the Fuhrer has never been revealed, as he was quickly hustled off to meet with Winston Churchill. Hess was sentenced as a war criminal in the Nuremberg trials and died in Spandau prison, and that mystery remains. I seem to have been gifted by God to have a good memory, and that gift was a great asset in my engineering career. Today it may be failing with daily events, but those childhood memories remain. Stories have been told of my being a problem child when in the teething process. Supposedly my grandmother would soak a wooden clothespin in Scotch, letting me suck on it to shut me up. ***"Whisky did something for Eddie Mackay from an early age."*** The early years of world war two were not easy for the people of Great Britain. The powerful Luftwaffe had been bombing the major cities on a nightly basis. While England suffered most destruction from those bombing raids, the Clydebank of Scotland was also a major target because of the shipbuilding facilities all along the River Clyde near Glasgow. In Ayrshire, we did receive some stray bombs, not being far from those major targets. As kids, we would travel all around the farm fields collecting pieces of shrapnel dug out of the craters from those stray bombs. Our village school was grossly overcrowded with kids evacuated from the Clydebank, where all the bombing was targeted. I was started in school in the summer of 1940 when my grandmother convinced the local school headmaster that I did not need to wait until the usual five years of age. Being considered a bright kid by many, I would skip the second grade. Going from first to third grade placed me in a class with kids older and physically larger. I did develop that *"small, but tough kid"* attitude in those childhood years. That cocky attitude to always be a winner, and top of the heap, stuck with me most of my adult life. Being that young bright kid placed among others older than myself is no doubt why I always felt I had to impress. I would proceed to High School at age eleven, graduating at the age of fifteen. Small, smart, and tough with a cocky attitude. In 1942 my mother was involved in a serious accident at the Troon shipbuilding facility when she had one arm torn off completely. She was operating a huge radial arm drilling machine putting holes in steel plates used for shipbuilding. This machine was an antique with none of the typical safety provisions. Every piece of equipment available was being used in the war effort. Having got a sleeve caught, she was dragged in and spun around like a rag doll. While unlucky, she was also fortunate that losing her left arm was the only significant bodily damage. Her whole body was badly bruised. A tough woman, she would now spend a lot of time reading and teaching me while she recuperated. She was an avid reader, managing to get books from many sources. Quite an accomplishment in those wartime days. My mother adapted to the loss of her arm very well, but there were two daily tasks she could not handle. They were the tying of her shoelaces and fastening the hooks of her bra. Those daily tasks were assigned to me for many years. I don't doubt that I was a spoiled child, having a loving mother, grandmother, and *"big sister like"* cousin, all living in a *"wee hoose"* in that village of Dundonald. Most of the kids were raised without fathers during wartime. Most able-bodied men and many women were enlisted in the armed forces, except for some employed in critical defense production. My grandmother was good friends with the Sheddon family, who operated a dairy farm about a mile from the village. This was considered an easy walking distance, and I would walk along with my grandmother when she would visit that farm. My grandmother was a seamstress and did lots of sewing jobs for many people. She was an expert at patching work clothes for everyone. That talent was appreciated in wartime, with new clothes being unavailable. The Sheddon family consisted of a mother, son, and two daughters, and they operated a typical dairy farm. Livestock consisted of Ayrshire dairy cows, some hogs, poultry, and lambs came from the north to fatten for market. Most of the fieldwork was done with draft horses consisting of six fine Clydesdales. There was also an old Fordson tractor, but fuel was rationed during those war years. Their car likewise did not go far due to petrol rationing. One older plowman assisted with the work as all the younger men were off to the war. I was put to work on that farm at the age of seven, becoming quite proficient with all tasks within my physical capabilities. I would go to the farm after school, and occasionally even before school. I stayed on the farm at weekends, and also during the summer when school was closed. John Sheddon would become my father- figure. He was one of the few young men working on a farm. His father was killed in an accident, allowing his exemption from military service due to critical farming needs. Schoolboys were used by all the farmers during those war years. In later war years, we had the German Prisoners of War help with the farm work. Two prisoners being dropped off early and picked up again in the evening. They were willing to help on the farm as opposed to staying in the prison camp. When the United States entered the war, they began shipping food supplies and all forms of military equipment in preparation for the invasion of Europe. This material was unloaded in the ports of the

river Clyde. Military tanks, trucks, and supplies were scattered all over the farm fields of Lanarkshire and Ayrshire. Everything was covered with camouflage netting awaiting travel south for the Normandy landings on D-Day. The netting was used to make this military equipment less conspicuous to the Luftwaffe bombers. This heavy equipment crushed the clay tile drainage pipes used throughout the farmland. Many fields were flooded and were untillable until being fixed after the war. My daily farming activities continued until I graduated high school at age fifteen. With my busy life of work and school, I then only assisted on some weekend occasions. After graduating from high school, I could have attended Glasgow University or the Glasgow Royal College of Science and Technology. Most people assumed I would choose the University. Tuition at both being free, but I did need to have enough money to live on. My mother was not in any position to support me. After the war, when my father had returned from the army, he and my mother were legally separated. Divorce was not permitted in Scotland, but a legal separation was allowed. Some people did move to England just to get divorced. My mother had gone to work full time in a shoe factory, and there were not many tasks that she could not handle with her one arm. She was quite ingenious at performing tasks and an exceptional individual in so many ways. Wages for women in Scotland were low, so our budget was always limited. My grandmother had died, and my sister had joined us at Dundonald. My two brothers continued to stay in Glasgow, not interested in becoming **"*country yokels.*"** I was living with my mother, cousin, and sister, sharing all expenses. I needed to go to work and have an income. My solution was to join Scottish Aviation as an indentured apprentice in aircraft engineering while attending Glasgow Tech. on a part-time basis. The normal workweek was five nine hours days. I was released one hour early on the three nights I attended the college that first year. With good grades, my second year was changed to one night per week and one day per week. With continued good grades, I was permitted to attend college an additional one week per month, making life much easier. I did complete that five years apprenticeship with Scottish Aviation on March 1st of 1957, also graduating from Glasgow Royal College of Science and Technology in June 1957. I was all set to head off to the United States as an aircraft engineer. I was convinced that I knew it all. The wee village of Dundonald had one church and two pubs. The legal drinking age was eighteen, but if one was in the workforce, then entering the pub at age sixteen was permitted, providing one behaved. My mother, Gertie Mackay, was a character and quite a drinker of beer and Scotch. She visited the local village pubs regularly, where her singing was always encouraged. I do believe her drinking would have been excessive, were she not protected by poverty. Drinking was a part of my early life with visiting the pubs at age sixteen. I was always known in the village pubs as ***"Gertie's boy."*** I was well accepted in the village pubs due to my ability as a fast scorekeeper of dart games. My numbers skill, no doubt, inherited from my father. Our drinking on weekdays was limited due to not having much money. Most of us young fellows would pool our resources, heading to town on weekends for drinking and dancing. We drank as much as we could afford. Drinking was considered a regular part of life, and it was expected of us. I always worked an additional part-time job to help with the expenses of our small household. Working part-time with a Kilmarnock landscape gardening company allowed me the opportunity to be the weekly gardener for ***Sir Alexander Fleming,*** inventor of penicillin. He had maintained the family home while spending his life in London. He always returned during summer months to the village of Darvel, where he grew up. His family home was maintained by a relative. Such an honor to meet this humble man that gave his life to research to help others. The city of Kilmarnock was significant, being the home of Barclay's Locomotive manufacturing facility. Barclay's locomotives were known throughout the British Empire when railroads and steam locomotives dominated all the transportation. Maybe more significant was the fact that Kilmarnock was the home of Johnnie Walker, born 1820 and still going strong. The bottling and blending of Scotch Whisky being a major source of employment and pride in that community. It was often said, ***"Whatever it did not kill, it took prisoner."*** Maybe I surrendered at an early age! The landscape gardening company where I was employed part-time maintained the gardens surrounding the Johnnie Walker's Headquarters buildings. My job was to take care of the many flowerbeds. I never imagined that Johnnie Walker Whisky would become my addiction. The area surrounding Kilmarnock was also known as the Burns Country. Our famous Scottish Bard, being born in Alloway, he farmed in Mauchline, close to Kilmarnock. I did some drinking in the Tam 'O Shanter pub in Ayr and the Poosie Nansie's pub in Mauchline. Both were made famous by Robert Burns. We were quick to quote Burns in saying ***"Whisky and Freedom Gang thegither."*** Drinking, telling stories, and singing in the local pubs, was a big part of trying to act like a grown-up in Scotland. Today my favorite quote from Burns is, ***"Life is but a day at most,"*** with it being similar to the A.A. quote ***"One Day at a Time."*** From a drinking young boy to a chronic alcoholic, finally to contented sobriety has been quite an interesting journey.

Myself, with my sister, mother, and cousin, before I departed from Scotland in 1957. The other picture with my mother was taken In 1977. One month before she would die so unexpectedly. An exceptional woman who passed on much too young

Dundonald Village with the Ancient Dundonald Castle

Tam O` Shanter Inn - Ayr, Scotland, since the 1700`s

Poosie Nansie`s Pub in Mauchline, Scotland, since the 1700`s

Chapter 16 - Having a Genetic Propensity -

My maternal grandmother and grandfather had come to Scotland from Cookstown, County Tyrone, in Northern Ireland. My grandfather worked in the steelworks in New Stevenson in Lanarkshire, while my grandmother was a seamstress. When my grandfather died of a heart attack, my grandmother relocated to the village of Dundonald, where her oldest daughter was living. She quickly became well known as a seamstress and as a maker of patchwork quilts. As a wee boy, I would often work the treadle of her sewing machine when her legs got too tired. She would tell me many stories of growing up as the oldest girl on that farm in Cookstown. Having to help her father in the butcher shop, and also with the daily chores of their small farm. Her father was considered quite a prominent citizen in Cookstown, being a farmer, butcher, and cattle dealer in that community. She would also tell of his regular drinking episodes on market day. After a good day at the weekly livestock market, her father usually got drunk. When it was time to close the pub, the owner would load her father into his pony cart, slap the pony on the butt, and it would take him home to the farm. Her mother, she described as a *"Holy terror."* When her father would get sober, her mother had him sign the pledge in the family bible, never to drink again. When he returned to the market, his habit of getting drunk was usually repeated. He had signed the pledge so often, there was no more space remaining in that family bible to register births, deaths, and marriages, as was the custom in those days.

  I do believe I may have had the genetic propensity to become an alcoholic. We can either die with alcoholism or from alcoholism. I am sure I will always be an alcoholic. **Active alcoholic, Recovered alcoholic, or Dead alcoholic**. Drinking, farming, and a hard-work ethic just seemed to come to me naturally. Genetic propensity, plus the environment of my upbringing in Scotland, may have contributed in some way to my alcoholism. I do believe that *"Eddie's contribution"* was the most significant factor. I am proud of my Scottish and Irish heritage, with so many strong traits, both good and questionable—*a recipient of many God-given talents.*

Scotland and Northern Ireland - Just 30 Miles by Ferry

Chapter 17 – A New Immigrant –

Leaving Prestwick Airport in Scotland, I arrived at New York's Idlewild Airport in June 1957. I was met by an aunt and uncle who were my sponsors, as required for entry to the United States. In Scotland, while in college and training as engineers, it was anticipated that many of us would emigrate to some other country to have a new life and career. Countries selected by many were Australia, New Zealand, South Africa, Canada, and the United States. All the countries except the U.S. were part of the British Empire, and it was easy to become a new citizen. The United States required a sponsor for entry, but it held more attraction to me with the fast-growing aircraft industry. My sponsor aunt was an older sister of my mother, who had come to the U.S. as domestic help when a young girl, she had married a German immigrant. They were dairy farmers in the Catskill region of New York State.

Since they acted as my sponsor, I agreed to work on their farm for that summer of 1957, before seeking employment in the aircraft industry. I was an energetic capable helper immediately due to my farming upbringing, my only problem being in trying to adjust to the heat. My uncle was a fine man and willing to keep me supplied with what I thought was weak beer, but it was cold. After the summer season, I proceeded to seek interviews for employment as an aircraft engineer. While it seemed my qualifications were excellent, my draft status was proving to be a problem. At that period, all immigrants were placed high on the list of local draft boards. I had been aware of being eligible for the draft but had not realized it would prevent companies from hiring me. I then took a job in plant equipment and layout engineering with Stanley Works in New Britain, Connecticut. I had come upon this job opportunity while being in East Hartford to interview with Pratt and Whitney. When arriving in Connecticut, I was fortunate to find a room for rent with a nice old English woman. She had one other room rented to a pretty schoolteacher from Gilmanton, New Hampshire. Later I would kid her about Gilmanton being the location of Peyton Place.
The book of that name by Grace Metalious was considered quite shocking in those times. We became close friends immediately, and she introduced me to the Congregational Church, which seemed somewhat similar to the Scottish Presbyterian Church. I was able to walk the half-mile to the Stanley Works, where my hard work ethic seemed well appreciated. Finding a bar after work was no problem, and after my first payday, I would become a daily drinker. I was only drinking a few beers after work but would never miss a day, and life was good. Not many individuals in Scotland could afford to be daily drinkers. Hartford, Connecticut, being the Insurance capital, attracted lots of young girls from Northern New England seeking clerical work. I was able to meet many of them quickly. They introduced me to a local ski club, with weekly meetings. When winter snow arrived, we headed to the ski slopes on the weekends. I quickly learned the techniques of this new sport, and I was fearless.

After the days of skiing, there was always drinking. I excelled in both being the life of the party. I did have a severe mishap on the slopes, having a shoulder separated by four inches. After getting it all fixed up, I had to undergo significant physical therapy, being unable to work for a brief period. While having this shoulder still in a sling, I was called for my military physical exam, being at the top of the draft board listing. Even with my obvious shoulder problem, my status was listed as (1A). They did place my enlistment date on delay, and I was required to furnish the draft board with updates of my physical condition. Later in early winter, when still not drafted, I decided to spend some time back on the farm in the Catskills, where I might do some skiing. I was then informed that my induction would be delayed until after New Year, and I would be drafted from New York State. I enjoyed spending time on the dairy farm doing regular chores. Also helping with cutting trees for lumber and for firewood used for heating the farmhouse. It was great outdoors work, and my uncle always kept me supplied with beer. I was in excellent physical shape when inducted into the U.S. Army at Fort Dix, New Jersey, on January 13$^{th\,of}$ 1959.

Chapter 18 – The United States Army –

My induction into the United States Army happened on January 13th1959, at Fort Dix, New Jersey. The beginning of another phase with many exciting experiences in my young life. After the usual army basic training, I received a primary Military Occupation Specialty (MOS) as a construction engineer due to my education. I was not required to undergo the usual advanced infantry training. Being provided with some military leave after that basic training, I had orders to report to the Special Warfare Center Headquarters in Fort Bragg, N.C. Arriving there April 1st. I discovered my MOS number of 811 had been misread. I had been assigned to a unit with requirements for MOS numbers of 810,812,813, and 814. My number of 811 belonged with the Construction Engineers.
Being informed that it may take some time to have this issue resolved, I would be required to do whatever was needed. This

Special Warfare Center consisted of both psychological warfare and guerrilla warfare divisions. Initially assigned to assist in the fabrication of signs and displays being produced for an educational exhibition at the upcoming Armed Forces Day in Washington D.C. My engineering printing skills were utilized along with my fabrication talents. Although only a low-life private, the officers were able to use my abilities effectively. Having more skills at age 25 than a typical 18-year-old inductee made it much easier to contribute to their preparation for this big event. Working with the Captain of the unit, he asked if I intended to have a career in the army, with my response being negative. He then stated that they could utilize my skills, and he could take care of whatever was required to keep me in his division. It seemed good to me. The closest city to Fort Bragg was Fayetteville, N.C., and this place opened my eyes to segregation in the United States. Although it was supposed to be integrated, there still existed segregated toilets and drinking fountains. What was most ridiculous were the segregated vending machines. Not my favorite city! My entire active duty was spent in the First Psychological Warfare Division, with my duties being varied, including being part of the teaching regime. I was in excellent physical shape, so army life was not difficult. Many of the draftees in my unit were college graduates with specialized skills. Many were educated in radio broadcasting and printed media. Many were artists and illustrators with experience in the advertising world. Mostly their skills applied to the unique requirements of this Special Warfare Center. I was the odd man out. Somehow my talents and engineering skills were found to be useful in this specialized unit of the U.S. Army. It was an educational two years, even although I had no interest in extending my military career.

Along with some slick con men in the unit, we could always find ways to make money from gambling to supplement the meager army pay. We did drink a lot of beer. I was also introduced to the North Carolina Moonshine. I achieved promotion to the rank of Specialist 4th Class, the highest level possible for a draftee. I was happy to be released from active duty in January 1961. While enlisted, I had pursued potential employment in the aircraft industry. I had made previous contacts when my draft status was my only problem. I was enthusiastic about a possible new career in the aircraft industry.

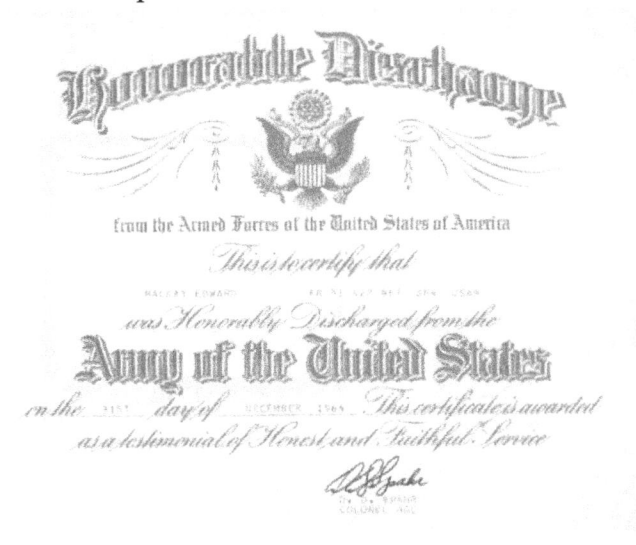

Chapter 19 – Truck Body Engineering -

Upon release from active duty in January 1961, I planned to accept a job offer from helicopter producer Kaman Aircraft, Bloomfield, Connecticut. My communication with them indicated my employment assured. I did feel that I could delay starting this job while I visited the farm in the Catskills. My idea was to possibly enjoy some skiing and she-ing. Two requirements of being separated from active military duty were to contact the local army reserve unit and the New York State Employment Office. The employment office insisted that I appear for an interview with *"Aerobilt Bodies,"* Athens New York, a subsidiary of Grumman Aircraft Engineering Corporation. This company produced aluminum truck bodies that were marketed exclusively by JBE Olson across the United States. I was quick to inform the first person to interview me on my plans to return to Connecticut for employment by Kaman Aircraft. They insisted on a complete review of my education, experience with Scottish Aviation, and work history, and seemed impressed. A fine gentleman named Harold Turner was the chief engineer. After I had spoken of my plans to do some skiing, he asked if I would consider taking a job temporarily. I did agree, with that temporary job, which would be continued for 34 years.

A new beginning of my automotive engineering career, and I did not have a clue as to what this job would entail. I did feel well equipped with strong basic skills in drafting, design, and education in engineering. I felt capable and well trained in aluminum design and fabrication with Scottish Aviation. I could take this new job and continue to live on the farm. Driving the 25 miles distance to work was easy, allowing my continued help on the dairy farm. The Catskills was a summer resort and a winter ski resort. Located some hundred thirty miles north of New York City. The city dwellers came by car and buses, with every resort having a bar with entertainment. Ideal location for a healthy young bachelor who loved to drink and party on weekends. Weekdays were strictly engineering and farm work, and my uncle always provided my daily supply of beer. The big new deal at that time was marijuana, with many people growing it locally. The smoke and marijuana smell was overwhelming when entering many of the bars, and it was a big attraction. Although never smoking tobacco in Scotland, I had started while in basic training in the army. I was smoking three packs per day of regular Camels by my time of separation from the army. Maybe my love for the Camels and the switching from beer to Scotch Whisky was enough, so I never tried smoking pot. Many friends offered, but I did not like the smell, and I was never to be tempted to try any other drug. The sixties were a crazy time in many ways. I was enjoying and experiencing a nice life as a young bachelor. Discharged completely from the US Army in 1965, after completing active and inactive reserve duties, was a relief due to the Vietnam war. The notorious Woodstock gathering of 1969 took place in the Catskill foothills just south of us. I thought those Hippies and dopers were crazy. In that year of 1969, I was more interested in the Lunar Landing as Grumman Aerospace was producing the Lunar Module known as the **"LEM."** I was a good student, and quickly understood the basic construction details of the Grumman aluminum Walk-In truck bodies. Becoming familiar with the Aluminum Data Book of alloys and mill products available for commercial use in the United States was a necessity. Understanding the numerous truck chassis variables would take much longer, but I was a good student. The aluminum walk-in truck body had been developed by Grumman Aircraft Engineering after the war in 1946. Original design and production were performed in Bethpage Long Island. When the post-war aircraft business grew, there was no space available, so truck body production had been relocated to Athens, NY. The necessary engineering functions had still been maintained at Bethpage. The creation of a local engineering department in Athens had been attempted without real success for anything other than existing body modifications. The market base was demanding upgrades in design, and Grumman had now hired Harold Turner, a known engineer in the school bus industry, and a real automotive engineer. Harold had been interested in my aircraft and aluminum design background, and I was eager to learn new skills. We related well from my first meeting. Before Harold Turner was hired, Grumman had contracted a new body design. This was done by one of their retired aircraft engineers, and he did an excellent job with a unique small *"Olsonette"* body design. This body had been mounted on a Ford half-ton stripped chassis, with a single wheelbase and a single body length. My initial task was to make this *"Olsonette"* body design available in additional body lengths with various wheelbases. A good beginner's task. I then proceeded to modify this body design for compatibility with a Chevrolet chassis with similar Gross Vehicle Weight Rating and wheelbases as the Ford chassis. Not too complex but challenging for a newcomer to this truck body business. I would proceed to handle many other assigned tasks, impressing Harold Turner with my skills and efforts. I never did consider the offer of employment made by Kaman Aircraft. I was excited to try this new life in the Catskills.

Harold Turner was a quiet-spoken gentleman, and I was a brash and mouthy young Scotsman. We had engineering minds as common ground. I do believe Harold was an engineering genius, and I had a mind like a sponge, ready to absorb his knowledge and expertise. I was honored when assigned the task of creating a new aluminum body design to replace the *"Kurbside"* body, created fifteen years prior by the Grumman Aircraft Engineers. Featured in that *"Kurbside"* aerodynamic design were roll-formed, stretch formed, and stamped aluminum components, along with aluminum sheet, extrusions using solid riveted assemblies. This new anticipated design would feature aluminum sheet with unique shaped extrusions and aluminum castings, with only formed components easily produced on a simple brake press. The solid riveted assembly techniques would remain. This design to cost less for tooling and have more flexibility. It would incorporate multiple body widths, heights, and lengths. Providing additional useable cubic load space to satisfy customer requirements. Similar overall length, height, and width with increased useable payload capacity. I certainly enjoyed the challenge and had superb guidance from Harold Turner. We delivered the prototype for review to a selected audience in New York City in June 1962. The response was varied, with many loving this new *"Kurbvan"* truck body. Many others would think it was extremely ugly. It had been designed to accommodate ease of manufacture with reduced costs, flexibility, and maximized useable cube space. Beauty was never a consideration. This was the beginning of *"Eddie Mackay and his ugly trucks."* A reputation that existed even when I had departed active truck body engineering. Form, fit, and function was my mantra, having smiled at my many critics through the years. With many of the major fleet customers, it was an instant success. Others claimed they would never purchase an *"Ugly Kurbvan Body."* Although easier to produce, it was not instantly appreciated by manufacturing. This newly designed body required manufacturing in the same facility that still produced the old *"Kurbside"* design. My success was both a blessing and a curse, but I was recognized and spoken of by many. Being naïve, I had anticipated eliminating the *"Kurbside"* body, which did not happen until many years later. It was hard to kill off that attractive aero style *"Kurbside"* truck body loved by many users. In the spring of 1963, Grumman would create a Grumman Allied Industries Division to include all commercial products, providing separation from the expanding defense and aerospace products. Commercial products included Grumman Canoes made in Marathon, New York, and Pearson Yachts in Portsmouth, RI. Since Grumman had now purchased the JBE Olson sales company, they changed the name of truck body manufacturing to Olson Bodies. Two additional manufacturing facilities would also be opened in Sturgis, Michigan, and Sherman, Texas. The Sturgis facility would initially assemble both truck bodies and canoes. Building the truck bodies in New York, Michigan, and Texas gave Grumman a significant advantage with national fleet users of Walk-In truck bodies. In addition to my engineering tasks, I would assist in the Sturgis start-up. This involved shipping the various truck body components and assemblies from Athens, New York, for final assembly in Sturgis, Michigan. An interesting new challenge for sure. Simultaneous start-up of truck body production was carried out in the Sherman Texas facility. Sherman, Texas, is located approximately an hour drive north of Dallas, close to Lake Texoma, which borders Texas and Oklahoma. This facility started with minimal problems due to the highly skilled labor force readily available. Being in the *"Baptist Belt,"* one had to join a club to be able to enjoy drinking whiskey. I was quick to become a member of all the liquor serving clubs in Sherman, Texas when I would visit there. I always enjoyed working with those easy-going and very productive employees of that facility. Many of these employees were also from farming backgrounds, being easy to relate to. I do not believe there was a heavy drinker in that whole workforce. They were typically two or three beers after work types. It was interesting that driving and drinking beer was allowed, and it was courteous when doing so, to drive on the wide shoulders. I think the Reagan Administration forced Texas to change that law with threats of cutting off Federal Highway Funding. Somehow when spending time in that Texas facility, my alcohol consumption was reduced, although never to the low levels of the locals. This was the only state where we had a presence that I was never stopped by law enforcement for some violation involving alcohol. This year of 1963 found me taking a fall vacation and heading to western Canada to visit two older brothers living in Calgary and Edmonton, Alberta. I had a sporty Chevrolet Corvair Spider car, making the trip from the Catskills to Calgary in four days of fast driving.

After spending time in Calgary with brother Tommy, I headed to Edmonton to see my older brother Garry. Also able to visit with many cousins that lived there. While returning to Calgary, I would receive an urgent phone call from a friend in New York. He informed me of the sudden death of my uncle, the dairy farmer. I was needed as soon as possible to assist with the daily milking of the dairy cattle. I caught a flight back to New York, with a friend of my brother promising to return my new car. My uncle had suffered a heart attack when returning from bowling. Shocking to all who knew him. I took a leave of absence from Grumman to handle the farm chores of the medium-sized dairy farm. With the silos full of ensilage and barns full of hay, it was decided to maintain the milking business through the winter, and my aunt and I did just that. With the Holstein dairy herd being considered of high quality, a special cattle sale was scheduled for spring. All the active milking cows were sold off, and we retained the calves and heifers. I now became a part-time farmer after returning to my job as a truck body engineer. This farm owned by my aunt consisted of 168 acres of hilly and wooded property, with good grazing and hay ground. I did have a crazy idea of turning the whole farm into a real challenging golf course. There were no existing golf courses in that region, and I was sure an excellent golf course would attract experienced golfers and beginners. I felt it may take a few years, but I did have that vision. Having grown up surrounded by some of the world's best golf courses in Scotland, my head and imagination were working overtime. My ultra-conservative aunt would not even allow the investigation of such a possibility. Just *"a pie in the sky idea"* was what she considered it. I did continue as a part-time farmer, providing adequate income from sales of veal calves and dairy replacement heifers to maintain the farm. It was necessary to surrender that role when starting to move engineering to Michigan in 1970. A neighbor farmer leased the farm, allowing my aunt to still have her home there. By that time, there were chintzy nine-hole golf courses all over that area. ***How ironic.*** Those years of farming and engineering kept me extremely busy, with daily drinking moderate, and mostly just beer. On weekends when able to do some skiing, then lots of Scotch would be consumed.

I also traveled frequently on engineering business, and more alcohol consumption became the norm. Harold Turner was well known in automotive circles and was active in the Society of Automotive Engineers. He encouraged me to join and become involved in the S.A.E., and I did that. I would accompany him to the many chassis engineering facilities across Michigan. He opened many doors to this brash young Scotsman. Automotive engineering in those times was indeed a drinking culture. I could drink excessive amounts and function quite well. There was often more work done at the bar and restaurant than took place during the regular workday. With JBE Olson's marketing and Olson Bodies, multiple facilities, the aluminum truck body usage expanded rapidly.

There was one other aluminum bodybuilder in the U.S. and over twenty regional steel body producers. After a couple of years, sales and manufacturing were combined under one name of Grumman Olson. Grumman Olson would quickly dominate the U.S. Walk-In truck body market. In 1966 we started to ship completed bodies assembled in Sturgis, Michigan, for mounting on General Motors chassis produced in Canada. This required setting up a local company in Oshawa, Ontario, to complete the assembly and

Installation. The finished products were then distributed throughout Canada by G.M. of Canada. They had a similar arrangement with Union City Body Company for steel Walk-in bodies. With the signing of the Auto Pact of 1968, we were able to produce completed units in Michigan and drive them across the border for distribution across Canada. It did not take long until the aluminum bodies would dominate the Canadian market within the G.M. distribution network. I made many trips to many locations across Canada. The Canadian Post Office would quickly appreciate the advantages of having standardized, high-quality postal delivery vehicles across that vast continent. We worked with their many various departments to assist in the creation of that uniform and productive Canadian Postal Delivery Unit.

Grumman Olson Body—Standard for Canada Post

Chapter 20 – The Making of a Package Car –

That so-called ugly *"Kurbvan"* body design had become well accepted by most users of Walk-In truck bodies. United Parcel Service as the largest customer, still refused to accept this design. They continued to use their favored *"Kurbside"* body. The U.P.S. *"Kurbside"* body had a load-space length of ten feet, with 400 Cu. Ft. available for packages. It was designated a P400 package car.

These Walk-In delivery trucks had various designations by different users. Called Milk-Wagons by some, and Pie- Wagons or Route-Trucks by many. U.P.S. had created the term *"Package Car."* They also added designations of P400, P600, and P800 to the bodies to indicate the cubic feet of load capacity.

The United Parcel Service company being started initially on the West Coast, soon expanded to the North East and Mid- Atlantic. In the sixties, the U.P.S. headquarters was located in their downtown Manhattan New York package facility. The new chairman of the board of this fast-growing and successful company had a strong desire to have a package delivery vehicle with a unique U.P.S. corporate image. They had typically purchased Package Cars from many regional bodybuilders. Grumman Olson now became a partner in the design and development of this unique U.P.S. body. In conjunction with the various departments of the U.P.S., Many concepts, ideas, and desires were reviewed and listed by importance by U.P.S. engineering. Grumman Olson engineering acted as a partner throughout this whole process. The U.P.S. engineer leading this effort was Ivan Pour, originally from Czechoslovakia. Before joining U.P.S., Ivan had experience with the Ward Motor Vehicle Company of Mt. Vernon, New York producer of electric delivery trucks and Walk-in bodies. Between Ivan Pour and Eddie Mackay, these concepts and wishes of so many resulted in a radical new *"Package Car."* A prototype body was assembled in Adam Black Body Shop, Jersey City. Located close to U.P.S. Headquarters. Mixed reactions were expressed by the U.P.S. groups at prototype preview. U.P.S. did decide to proceed with formal engineering and documentation of this new design. This first crude P600 prototype unit was then transferred to the Grumman Olson facility in Athens, NY. Complete detailed design and documentation being finalized by Grumman Olson Engineering. It was agreed that Grumman Olson would furnish engineering drawings to U.P.S. These drawings with Grumman Olson in the title block could not be used by any other manufacturer. U.P.S. would be required to copy this detailed information to U.P.S. titled drawings to allow this design to be produced by other bodybuilders. U.P.S. added drafting staff to their engineering department to complete this task.

Real production of this new P600 body mounted on a Ford chassis began in 1965, followed shortly by a larger P800 model. While Grumman Olson was the initial body producer, they were soon followed by Mark Body Company in Detroit and Adam Black Body Company in New Jersey. This body design was quickly nicknamed *"The Brown Bomber."* The rapid growth of the U.P.S. caused new distribution centers to be opened across the United States. These facilities were being furnished with the latest design, *"Brown Bomber."* It was soon recognized as synonymous with the fast delivery of packages. Most of the distinctive features introduced in this design still exist in the current version of the *"Brown Bomber"* seen in operation today. This was another design that was driven by form, fit, and function, and certainly did not win any beauty contest. That U.P.S. engineer, Ivan Pour, a vodka drinker from Czechoslovakia, and Eddie Mackay, a Scotch drinker from Scotland, would continue to work together for many years until Ivan's retirement. Both were well recognized in the automotive circles of greater Detroit. Ivan Pour was also the voice of ***Radio Free Europe,*** broadcasting to audiences behind the Iron Curtain from the annual S.A.E. International Convention in Detroit. During that week-long event each February, we rarely drew a sober breath. That was when Detroit was Motown. In later years U.P.S. expanded to Germany. A German bodybuilder was set up to produce this design mounted on a Daimler Benz chassis. This was an opportunity for Ivan Pour and Eddie Mackay to take the aluminum truck body design with its many improvements to Germany. Their delivery vehicles were very much lagging concerning the driver's ease of ingress and egress. This was a significant feature of the "Walk-In-Van" with the so-called Bar-Stool driver's seat. This seating arrangement and sliding door facilitated operator ingress and egress. Essential for efficient multi-stop deliveries.

Harold Turner and Eddie Mackay of Grumman Olson, discuss design concepts with Ivan Pour of United Parcel Service

Combining the ideas from many, to create a unique truck body design which is still in evidence today after 35 years of service

The Brown Bomber - A given Nickname to a truck that would become easily recognized – A Well Proven Winner

1956 Aorobilt Bodies Kurbside U.P.S. P400
(Now a Display Unit)

A U.P.S. P600 in Munich Germany

Chapter 21 – Advancements at Grumman -

A significant outcome of my involvement with the U.P.S. in creating their body design with improved features was a new Grumman Olson body designated the *"Kurbmaster."* This enhanced 1968 replacement for the *"Kurbvan"* featured a large front hood, with more access to facilitate routine service. Another later designed *"Kabmaster"* would provide even more access to chassis and powertrain components for ease of maintenance. Making these ongoing improvements was mandatory, with vehicle maintenance costs increasing. We were always willing to listen to inputs from the national fleets along with smaller retail users. That was the key to our success. Form, Fit, Function, and durability, not style or beauty, motivated our design efforts. Grumman management decided in 1970 that truck body design engineering should be relocated to the Sturgis Michigan facility. This would provide closer proximity to the greater Detroit area and all of the major chassis manufacturers. Harold Turner being close to retirement, would not consider relocation. I certainly loved the Catskill region and my great way of life there. To continue my career with Grumman Olson, I had to accept the challenge of relocating the engineering department. We had previously established a limited engineering department in Sturgis, having problems finding a strong leader. This relocation project required me to spend significant time in Sturgis. My task was made more difficult due to my assisting in the startup of a new truck production facility in Tulare, California, in the San Joaquin valley. I was now living between New York, Michigan, and California, and working endless hours. While enjoying the challenges and responsibilities, my drinking did escalate to new levels. Most of this being at company expense, and I was living like a gypsy. Traveling between New York, Michigan, and California with a garment bag and a briefcase. I had a new home in a lake cottage in Michigan, and still my home at the farm in the Catskills. The farmland had been leased to a neighbor providing limited income for my aunt. That new truck body plant located in

California's San Joaquin valley in 1970 was built from scratch, and I enjoyed being able to provide my input. The city of Tulare is located in that productive valley, where everything grows when water is added. Water rights are more important than land rights. I was fascinated with the diversity of agriculture in that valley. That was the location of the first extensive production dairy farm facilities, and I did spend time marveling at these operations. The dairy farms all seemed to be owned by Portuguese, while operated by imported Dutch immigrants. It is one hot place. For our grand opening of that new Tulare manufacturing facility, we had invited our west coast and mid-west salesmen, along with many major existing customers and potential new customers.

An evening of dining and drinking followed in Visalia, ten miles north of Tulare. Departing that heavy drinking session to return to the motel in Tulare, I was stopped by the California Highway Patrol for making an illegal U-turn. While they checked my license, I was subjected to routine sobriety tests. I was doing well until I was requested to stand on one leg while they continued with their questions. Then when asked by the trooper to switch legs, I keeled right over, feeling stupid and ridiculous as I tried to regain my upright position. I did convince them that I had an early morning flight scheduled back to New York, and they decided to let me go, conditional on my being on that flight. I did continue to stay in Tulare another week, but only did my drinking locally. When back in New York and Michigan, I would introduce this **"California Sobriety Test"** to my drinking friends. An unheeded warning became barroom fun. This was the early stages of what would become my chronic alcoholism

Chapter 22 – New Products, Marriage, and Travels -

I did manage to make the trip to Scotland for a vacation in 1971. My first return since leaving in 1957, it was nice to be treated as the wee village boy with success in America. My relocation from the Catskills to Michigan was completed by 1972, where I had purchased a lovely lake cottage. We had also started production of a newly designed Motor Home in 1970 in the Sturgis facility. With an increase in truck body sales, the lack of factory floor space available for this Motor Home production became a problem. Motor Home production was then transferred to our Pearson Yachts facility in Portsmouth, RI. This caused additional traveling to assist with this new production startup. Grumman would then open another new manufacturing facility in 1972 in Montgomery, PA, for the production of modular buildings. With extra space being available in this facility, the motor home production was now transferred from Rhode Island to Pennsylvania, with still more traveling required. During those days of long working hours and so much travel, my daily drinking was not too excessive. Occasional heavy drinking episodes did seem to occur. Having Sturgis as a home base found me in a serious relationship with a beautiful woman named Patricia Hinckley. Patricia, a divorcee, had a son and daughter, both teenagers, and we were married in 1974. I had also been promoted to the position of chief engineer with the retirement of Harold Turner in 1974. A new life in marriage and added engineering management created new challenges. In this management role, I would receive lots of guidance from a great friend Bill Snyder, general manager of the Sturgis truck production facility. Bill had a great talent when working with people, and he was quick to nudge me in the right direction as a manager. He could provide gentle criticism and the right suggestion when needed. We became close friends as he became my new mentor, with the absence of Harold Turner. Before my marriage, I was motivated to fix up and redecorate that lake cottage. I also brought my mother from Scotland for a vacation and my wedding with Patricia. A busy, enjoyable life for sure. Transition and adapting to the responsibilities of married life came easy to me. Patricia and I were undoubtedly well suited. She was a McCreery with Irish ancestry and was extremely tolerant of my drinking, which I had reduced somewhat. I would still indulge in excess when out of town on business, and especially in Detroit. Patricia would become more concerned later with my increased body weight. She was, however, still extremely tolerant of my overindulgence. With the inability to satisfy the U.P.S. truck body needs, Grumman Olson purchased a small facility in Mayfield, PA, in 1974, dedicating it solely to U.P.S. P600 and P800 body production. Initially, the components for these truck bodies were produced by the Athens and Sturgis plants, with the final assembly being completed at Mayfield. More travel for Eddie Mackay, assisting with another production startup. The U.S. oil crisis in 1974 had caused the cessation of Motor Home production, which was switched over to Mini-Bus bodies. This bus body design could use many similar body components, being mounted on the identical chassis. Different products with different end-users from walk-in truck bodies. This required different design engineering with more new challenges. For many years Grumman Olson had furnished New York City with small truck bodies which had then been converted into ambulances by a facility in Manhattan. The ambulance and rescue vehicle body business had now expanded, and we proceeded with a new ambulance body design to be manufactured in the Sturgis facility. Different products, specialized needs, and other customers, with these new bodies being mounted on a Cab Chassis produced by Ford and General Motors. Another learning curve with additional challenges. We developed an excellent quality product. Grumman had also purchased a fire engine truck company in Indiana, relocating that manufacturing to Roanoke VA. The decision to transfer the ambulance body products to be combined with the fire and rescue truck bodies seemed logical, with ambulance bodies having similar end-users. Once more, I was designated to assist in the transfer of that ambulance body product line from Sturgis, MI, to Roanoke VA. Another occasion for increased indulgence in Johnnie Walker at company expense.

Chapter 23 - Dundonald Farm –

While living in the lake cottage near Sturgis, the lake was quite crowded with weekenders from Chicago in the summer months. I had a real desire to find a small farm property. With my wife

Patricia working at selling real estate, she was assigned that task. In the fall of 1977, she located a neglected old farmhouse with old barns and 34 acres between Centreville and Three Rivers, Michigan. Coming to look around the old farm, with Prairie River running through the property, it was an instant *"Must Have"* for Eddie. We were able to complete the purchase before heading off to Scotland for our vacation. I had planned to take Patricia to see God`s most incredible creation called Scotland. We toured the whole country except for the Islands. Shortly after that wonderful vacation, we needed to return to Scotland. My mother had died suddenly of a ruptured stomach ulcer. Living alone, by the time she had been discovered, there was too much damage. That exceptional woman passed on to another world. I was shattered with the passing of that seemingly indestructible woman. She was always singing, laughing, and taking care of everyone else. Patricia and I had teamed up with my brothers Garry and Tommy in Toronto for the flight to Prestwick airport, which was six miles from the village of Dundonald. We drank our way across the Atlantic, getting a rental car to take us home to Dundonald. We indeed did the best we knew how to give her a great send-off. The wake and funeral were drinking events. My mother was well known in many areas and organizations across Scotland and Northern Ireland. Her life of singing and giving to all in need was certainly well remembered by many. On our return from Scotland, we moved into the old farmhouse. I thought it should be demolished to allow for new home construction. Patricia had a desire to restore that century-old house, and she made the final decision. It was like camping out that winter, starting with restoration in spring. It would have been nice to maintain the lake cottage as a rental property. Financial needs for restoration of the farmhouse dictated the sale. When Patricia had visited Scotland, she was fascinated with the wee village of Dundonald. The grand old Dundonald Castle was on the hill above the main street, where I had grown up. She had also visited the Newfield Farm, where I spent so much of my childhood. I had told her so much of my life in those wartime years. As soon as we moved into that old ramshackle apple farm, Patricia labeled it *"Dundonald Farm."* That name is well known by many today. Patricia had also fallen in love with the beautiful Scottish Highland cattle that we observed while touring the Scottish Highlands. I had procrastinated, never getting around to buying any Highland Cattle to have them grazing on Dundonald Farm before Patricia`s death. In my new sobriety, along with my new farming way of life beginning in 1995, I was quick to locate and purchase five Highlands. This action being precipitated as one of my ***ninth step amends to Patricia***. Never having known about moderation in my lifetime, more Highland Cattle were soon being added to the original five head. I would quickly need more acreage for grazing. A good neighbor willingly allowed grazing on eight adjacent acres that he was unable to irrigate for crop farming. I was now in beef cattle farming, along with my continued flock of sheep with the increase in numbers.

Dundonald Farm 1977—Neglected Old Apple Farm

Chapter 24 - Progressive Alcoholism -

I had been appointed Vice President of Engineering in 1978. Now being a corporate officer of Grumman Corporation, I was humbled. Also nervous about the additional responsibilities. Adapting to the increased demands in engineering management was challenging. My daily drinking was moderate, and weekend drinking was usually in the company of my wife, Patricia, and not too excessive. Occasional heavy drinking happened, generally, while on business travels. I had been arrested for drinking and driving in both Pennsylvania and Ohio. Deals had been negotiated with authorities with paying of fines and receiving warnings. Previously when arrested in Sturgis in 1972, it was my first experience with the new breathalyzer machine. It registered a BAC of 0.18 when the limit was 0.15. I was barely over the limit. I had a New York driver license and Michigan License plates. I received a warning and ultimatum to get a Michigan Driver license. Later arrests for drinking and driving in Michigan bothered my wife Patricia much more than they did me. On one occasion, when arrested, the breathalyzer indicated a BAC 0.28 and 0.34. I had the results thrown out since testing requires the two outputs to be within two points. The deputy sheriff was not adequately trained to administer the test. In 1986 when arrested again with high BAC, I did receive a driver license restriction. This also required attendance at Alcoholic Awareness Sessions. Being sentenced to probation for a period, I had no problem convincing the probation officer, this was an occasional mishap. Negotiating a deal at any price, I kept on drinking and driving.

No doubt living in delusion. Unaware of the severity of my problem. The insidious problem with alcoholism is that unpredictable progression. I do remember having a blackout when I was young in Scotland. Occasional blackouts continued through the years. The blackouts became more frequent with longer duration. They were unpredictable and scary but never frightening enough to reduce my drinking. On one occasion, before giving an oral presentation at the S.A.E. International Convention, I was reviewing my notes at breakfast. Some attendees from Germany requested they join me for breakfast. They then congratulated me on an outstanding presentation. It seemed I made that presentation in a blackout on the previous day, having no recollection. Real scary, but I bluffed with ease. We had a good engineering discussion of my topic on areas to consider using aluminum components for weight reduction. I didn`t discuss my blackouts openly until my second year in recovery.

Not sure if I was afraid or embarrassed to discuss my blackouts. Other things would also surface. George Weller told me not to worry, as I would talk about such happenings when I became ready. He said our past could be compared to an old turd-bucket that had skinned over. Stirred up, it will surely stink. Our alcoholism was progressive, and our recovery needs to be progressive. As we become spiritually fit, we can address these areas of our past that have been suppressed for survival. One scary event was when driving one morning, I realized I was 20 miles from home when I should have been in Pontiac.

I was staying at a Pontiac hotel while meeting with G.M. engineers. After an evening of dining and drinking with the G.M. engineers, I wanted more alcohol. Instead of returning from some bar to my hotel, I had headed home in a blackout. I quickly turned around that morning, drove back to Pontiac, got cleaned up, and made the scheduled meeting on time. On another occasion, when driving home one Friday evening in a blackout, I failed to stop at a dead-end, crashing into a fence. This resulted in the loss of my upper teeth and a cracked jaw bone. I was right there at work on Monday morning, no matter how bad I looked. How did I survive and not kill some innocent person? In the months before going to Hazelden, I frequently checked the pots and dishes in the morning to see what I had for supper. I accepted my blackouts, adjusting my life to live with them. On occasions at work, when a topic was brought up, and I did not have a clue, I just listened and acted like I was aware. Eventually catching up with whatever the discussion entailed. In my working hours, I was sharp, alert, and extremely productive. I was fooling the engineering world and myself. I believe my functioning alcoholic way of life was a learned process. I was a good student.

Chapter 25 – U. S. Post Office Electric Vehicles -

That year of 1978 was also significant with new engineering challenges. Due to the recent energy crisis, the U.S. Postal Service expressed a serious interest in using electric-powered vehicles to deliver the mail. The history of our dealings with the U.S. Post

Office had not been positive. They had continued to purchase the low-priced steel-bodied delivery vehicles. They would give lip service to the potential change to aluminum truck bodies. Their delivery trucks had a life of five years before being scrapped. They corroded quickly in what is known as the ***"Rust Belt"*** of the U.S. These postal delivery trucks traveled extremely low mileage, with the typical unit averaging 5000 miles per year. Grumman management perceived the development of an aluminum-bodied electric vehicle for postal delivery service as a new opportunity to expand existing product offerings. Although comfortable and competent in aluminum body design, this project would involve a complete vehicle design, and that seemed a significant task to undertake. I was fortunate to have assembled an engineering team with varied skills and experience, and I was always ready to accept any challenge. The president of Grumman Corporation felt strongly about alternate energy sources. I did not doubt we would have real support in our efforts. Electric Delivery trucks were not a new idea. I had recalled the electric milk delivery trucks in Scotland, sometimes called Milk Floats. Ward Motor Vehicle Company, Mount Vernon N.Y. had produced many electric delivery trucks with United Parcel Service being a prominent user before 1960

Limited range and battery weight was a problem and a challenge. Our initial design ideas favored front-wheel drive, providing more storage space for batteries in the rear area. It was also decided to utilize commercially proven components wherever possible. In looking toward small front-wheel-drive automobiles, the V.W.-Rabbit looked like a candidate with proven drive train components. At the urging to stay with domestic manufacturers, we decided to use drive components from a Ford Fiesta. The design and production of our prototype unit was completed in late 1978. Testing and demonstrations were ongoing in 1979. A more efficient electric motor and battery configuration was installed in a second prototype with substantial improvement. This second vehicle also complied with the U.S.P.S. and D.O.E. requirements. With V.W. having begun production of V.W.-Rabbit with diesel engine in Westmoreland PA, we decided to switch front wheel drive components from Ford Fiesta to V.W. Rabbit, with heavier axle weight rating. Vehicle number three incorporated front-wheel-drive of the V.W. Rabbit, and rear axle of V.W.-Dasher, providing the needed increase in payload capacity.

  We would continue to work closely with U.S.P.S. engineering, and they did purchase ten Kurbwatt electric vehicles for a test program in Evansville, Indiana. A bid request from U.S.P.S. for 375 electric trucks had been anticipated in 1979 but never materialized. The U.S.P.S. did finally procure 31 E.V.'s in 1983, which were operated successfully in Cupertino, California. A few Kurbwatts were sold, with Long Island Lighting Company acquiring six units in 1984. Later donating them to major universities. The energy crisis had passed, and likewise, the pursuit of alternative-energy vehicles. Returning to the dependable and familiar gas-guzzling trucks. It was said of the E.V.'s, they could take you anywhere you wanted to go, they just may not bring you back home. I drove one of our prototype Kurbwatt minivans daily for some time. Frequently it would be abandoned at some drinking establishment, having to be towed back to our production facility. We were quick to add tow hooks to the front as they were frequently used.

Chapter 26 - Diesel Minivan to Long Life Vehicle

Having this new mini-van body already designed for the electric vehicle, it was an obvious candidate for conversion to a new diesel-powered delivery truck. A speedy test program was completed, and there was a definite market interest for this all-aluminum unitized construction 100 cubic foot capacity vehicle named *"Kubvan."* Chrysler has claimed to have introduced the first minivan in 1984, and that was a year after the Grumman Olson Kubvan was introduced in Detroit. The actual first probably the Chevrolet Corvair Greenbrier of the sixties. Production of these Kubvan units with V.W. diesel and drive components began in the Grumman Montgomery PA facility. It was anticipated that this unit could be tailored to comply with the revised U.S.P.S. requirements, and we had been working very closely with the U.S.P.S. engineering team. In 1983 the U.S.P.S. had decided to combine their current ¼ ton and ½ ton vehicles into an entirely new unit. It was designated the Long-Life Vehicle (LLV), and they created a preliminary specification. Performance and durability requirements to demonstrate a 12-year powertrain and 24- year body life being highlights of this LLV vehicle. This specification also included an unleaded gas engine, eliminating any consideration of our diesel-powered Kubvan unit. We then began working with Ford Motor Company, acquiring the pre-production release of gas-powered front wheel drive components. These new components would be released later with the Ford Tempo/Topaz product offerings. The early prototypes of this new gasoline-powered *"Kubvan"* were well received, with test units put into service with G.T.E. These G.T.E. units were used as special repair vehicles, resulting in lots of positive feedback. U.S.P.S. finally released a detailed specification in 1984. After review and many informal discussions, it appeared that the specifics of the detailed tire chain clearance requirement would eliminate the use of any front-wheel-drive configuration. These latest specifications dictated a traditional body on rear wheeled drive chassis configuration. The current supplier of steel-bodied units to the U.S.P.S. was A.M. General Corporation. We now became aware that they already had a prototype configuration in advanced stages. It now seemed obvious that they had a significant head-start with this U.S.P.S. Long Life Vehicle design. We proceeded to research what existing rear-wheel-drive chassis may be a candidate for modification to accept a body that would meet this new U.S.P.S. specification. The Chevrolet S10 Blazer vehicle appeared to have a basic chassis with the potential for modification. We then initiated conversations with General Motors as a possible partner. General Motors had no interest in being a prime contractor to U.S.P.S. They were willing to provide major components that were available within their various divisions. A small team of G.M .engineers was assigned to work with Grumman Olson to pursue the possibility of a unique new vehicle using a G.M. chassis and Grumman Olson Body. This unit would be designated the Grumman /GM LLV. This was now our third effort in creating a candidate vehicle for this upcoming U.S.P.S./LLV bid request. I felt more at ease with the concept of an aluminum body mounted on a G.M. chassis. I had been doing this successfully for years. This G.M. engineering team were all new individuals to get acquainted with, and they were a pleasure to work with. The final chassis was an S10 Blazer converted to right-hand- drive. Powered with a 4-cylinder Iron Duke engine and automatic transmission from G.M. of Strasbourg, France, also having a wide track rear axle. While this was a new unique, completed chassis assembly, the individual components were all proven within various General Motors Divisions. In our ongoing involvement with the U.S.P.S. engineering and procurement individuals, it did seem that we were probably the least favored candidate. There was no doubt that the A.M. General Corporation was the front runner. Others were being invited to legitimize this large procurement of their Long-Life Vehicle for postal delivery. A severe test protocol to demonstrate durability and performance duty cycle had been released by the U.S.P.S. This durability test of 24000 miles included various events that were considered extremely tough by normal automotive standards. Compliance and completion of these tests were necessary before the submission of the price and production proposal. What seemed like an indication that this may be a fair competition based on real performance, not politics, was the inclusion of a team from Booz Allen Hamilton as independent consultants. This team would join with the U.S.P.S. engineering group to monitor the testing of all of the Technical Proposal Vehicles. The test facility chosen was the Uni-Royal Proving Ground in Laredo, Texas. Three Test Proposal Vehicles were submitted by the A.M. General Division of LTV Aerospace, POVECO, a new corporation formed by General Automotive Group and Fruehauf Trailer Corporation, and the Grumman Olson Division of Grumman Allied Industries. Test Proposal Vehicles were now driven and subjected to all the various challenging events for 20 hours per day. This allowed for routine maintenance and vehicle checks between 2.00 am and 6.00 am daily. The Grumman unit was available for this torture track testing, 99.5% of the allotted time. All systems operated in a manner that would impress the consultants, U.S.P.S., and the Uniroyal professional test track employees. This was truly an amazing success, with a lot of the credit owed to our partners from General Motors. They had insisted that we start testing a prototype at the G.M. Proving Ground in Mesa, Arizona, before submission of the Test Proposal Vehicle (TPV) to the Laredo test track. They had also duplicated the test track events from the proposed Laredo testing on to the test track in Mesa. This test was still ongoing as we began the testing in Laredo. We were able to identify some areas of concern at body chassis attachments on the test unit being operated at Mesa. The U.S.P.S. did permit us to install the required reinforcements to the TPV unit at the Laredo track, providing it was accomplished during the four hours daily service period. Successful testing of this Grumman/GM LLV- Test Proposal Vehicle was completed on April 28[th]1985, at that Uni-Royal Laredo Test Facility. Competing vehicles from the other two participants had numerous failures on the track. U.S.P.S. being lenient in allowing numerous fixes and modifications to both of these units. They did even allow a total vehicle replacement of the POVECO TPV unit. We felt that disqualification was appropriate, had the testing requirements of the U.S.P.S. been truly observed. Politics and favored A.M. General Corporation, along with a desire for competitive bids, prolonged this test phase. Nearly a year would pass after the successful completion of the Grumman/GM LLV unit before the USPS would finally make an award. On April 8[th]1986 Grumman Allied were awarded the contract to produce **99,150 U.S.P.S. LLV`s** with delivery to be completed in January 1993. This award was for **$1.155,196,650.00**. An additional contract was then awarded before completion, and the production of LLV`s continued at a rate of 400 units/week through 1995. This was certainly a highlight in my engineering and management career. The design team leader on this LLV project was also the first female engineer I had ever hired, and she was an extremely talented engineer. Leading the design and assembly effort required to produce and test those early prototypes, plus the Test Proposal Vehicle was a significant accomplishment. With the limited time available, most of this effort was accomplished without formal engineering in our engineering development facility. This effort entailed seven days per week with many long hours, with plenty of alcohol being consumed by myself. Maintaining ongoing liaison with the G.M. team also required lots of travel, with more excessive consumption of alcohol. It could easily have been said that Eddie Mackay was a highly functioning alcoholic. It did take some additional years before anyone even suggested that I may have a serious problem with alcohol. There is no doubt that I was living in delusion, with my loving wife being the only person expressing real concern. She continued to be tolerant, and I still wonder why. So many successes in engineering made it difficult when arriving in Hazelden to admit that my life was unmanageable. I was two people, with one managing my engineering career, the other managing my alcoholism. By the time I reached Hazelden, management of my alcoholism had become a fulltime job. I was living under the lilacs, believing all was well. I can still smile some when thinking of that day of April 8[th]1986 in Washington D.C. Grumman had just received that **$1,155,196,650.00** award for production of **99,150 U.S.P.S. LLV delivery trucks.** The Postmaster General was lavishing compliments regarding the outstanding performance of the Grumman/GM TPV on that tough Laredo track. He then proceeded to say that he considered this vehicle to be *"extremely ugly,"* with some hope that the appearance could be improved. With my cocky attitude, I responded, ***"there was no mention of beauty in the request for proposal, but after 20 years in service, they will get to look very pretty".*** Wherever I travel today, I can still see that **ugly postal vehicle,** making deliveries after 30 years of service. Maybe it is true that beauty is in the eyes of the beholder. Quite an accomplishment for a highly functioning alcoholic, supported by so many dedicated individuals. It is quite scary to reflect. I did not have a clue how far my alcoholism had progressed. My *"Guardian Angels"* were still working overtime.

**SUNDAY APRIL 28, 1985 @ 3:00 P.M.
GRUMMAN/GM LLV/TPV
SUCCESSFUL COMPLETION OF
USPS 24,000 MILE DURABILITY TEST AT
UNI-ROYAL, LAREDO, TEXAS**

This U.S.P.S Team were an exceptional group of dedicated individuals who monitored all of the vehicles submitted for this 24,000 miles durability test

Chapter 27 - More Product and More Alcohol -

Production of the postal vehicles would be performed at the Montgomery PA facility of Grumman, now created as a separate LLV Division of Grumman Allied Industries. This decision caused the cessation of the *"Kubvan"* minivan production. Many who had worked so hard in the creation of this all-aluminum unitized minivan were disappointed. I do still own one of the *"Kubvan"* models powered by the Ford Tempo power unit, and front-wheel-drive installed in that aluminum structure. It is still used for local travel, and while over thirty years old, it will run for many more years. Those years of the 1980s were hectic in our engineering department. In addition to minivans powered by electric, diesel, and gasoline, and the challenge of satisfying the postal service, we also designed, developed, and tested a unique all-aluminum unitized fifth-wheel trailer. This new product was designed specifically for the transportation of potato chips for Frito Lay. This fifth-wheel trailer was towed by a Grumman Olson *"Krew Kab"* tow unit. Frito-Lay decided to utilize these large capacity trailers to distribute snack foods to regional locations for further distribution by conventional route trucks and large volume deliveries. This *"Krew-Kab"* tow unit with *"Kubemaster"* fifth-wheel trailer had required extended durability and performance testing at the Bendix Automotive Proving Grounds, in New Carlyle, Indiana, and at the Ford Arizona Proving Grounds. Production of these units was terminated after a short period in service due to driver licensing requirements. Many states insisted on drivers of these vehicles having a Commercial Driver's License, just like drivers of Class 8 truck trailers. A typical route truck driver only required an operator driver's license. The hiring of premium paid operators with CDL's would prove cost-prohibitive, so this great concept of Frito Lay was abandoned. This engineering and production effort proved to be a costly engineering effort with no payback. The 1980s provided many engineering challenges with rewards and frustrations. Being at the forefront and a strong leader, I would always show that cocky, confident, and capable attitude. Some of these tasks were stretching my skills and capabilities in both engineering and management fields. This is when my daily consumption of Johnnie Walker would begin to increase significantly.

Along with more alcohol came more weight gain and the beginning of negative physical changes to a previously healthy body. My mind was probably also affected much more than I would ever admit. Legal problems were indeed an annoyance, causing my wife much more concern than myself. I now believe alcoholism is a powerful disease that can convince any person that it can be managed. No matter how many harmful incidents caused by blackouts and lack of control, the daily indulgence, rationalization, justification, and flawed thinking would prevail. I was well-traveled along that path of self-destruction. With the tragic and unexpected demise of my loving wife Patricia in December 1989, that destructive lifestyle would reach a new level. It amazes me that I could continue to function in my capacity as V.P. of engineering with my increased daily consumption of alcohol. There is no doubt that alcohol did something for me in my younger years. Now with the progression of my alcoholism, it was doing a lot more to me—an intelligent, talented, and logical engineer living in delusion.

Alcoholism is an insidious and powerful disease

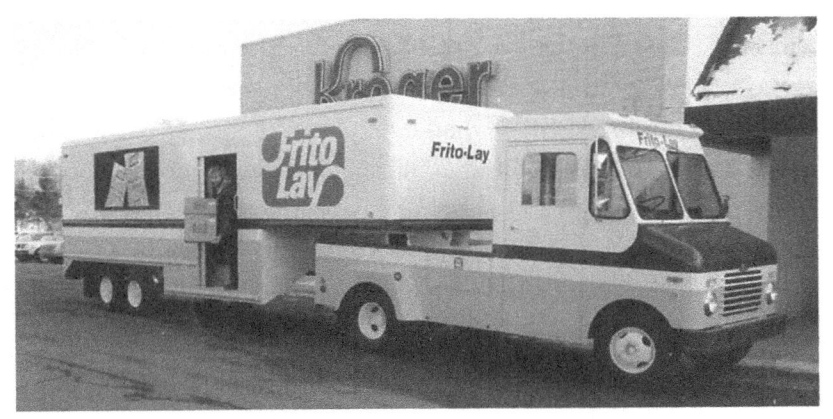

Krew-Kab Walk-In Tow Unit and Kubemaster Unitized Aluminum Trailer Combination—A Noble Experiment

Chapter 28 - The Deutsche Bundespost –

Recognition of our success with the new postal vehicle was not restricted to the United States. The Deutsche Bundespost in Germany was also considering the standardization and procurement of efficient delivery vehicles. We had been invited to meet and discuss the possibility of having our type of Walk-In truck body considered as a candidate for their future use. We did have a previous relationship with Daimler-Benz starting in 1970 when they imported chassis to the United States. That effort had been abandoned, but later in the 1980s, they produced chassis in the U.S., which would accept Grumman Olson bodies. On my previous trips to Germany, I was aware that most delivery truck bodies were being manufactured by small local body-builders. They looked like the bodies of the U.S. in the 1950s. There had been little advancement for ease of driver entry and egress. We had assisted U.P.S. in having their ***"Brown Bomber"*** P600 truck body produced in Germany by Willy Spiers Body Company. Initially, we had shipped over components for assembly in Germany. With some assistance, they were soon able to produce a complete delivery truck vehicle. Those package delivery trucks were now being observed across Germany with their many attractive features. This new interest in future market potential in Europe led to discussions with many producers of chassis. I did visit the Iveco Chassis Headquarters in Italy, but nothing materialized in Europe. We started installing bodies on the Iveco chassis in the U.S. We had established a strong partnership between Grumman Olson and General Motors of Europe, located in Russelsheim, Germany. This being easier due to the Grumman / General Motors' success with the U.S.P.S. A condition of inclusion as a bidder in the Bundespost Request for Proposal for anticipated multi-year procurement would require submission of ten prototype units for their evaluation. These units would require total compliance with their new specifications. Working closely with General Motors of U.S. and General Motors of Europe, along with engineers of the Deutsche Bundespost, we assembled ten special units for delivery to Germany. Quite a challenge since these vehicles required approval by a German Agency called TUV. This agency reviews vehicles for compliance with applicable German safety standards and emissions requirements. My safety engineer worked diligently, satisfying this compliance. Our lack of language skills did not make the task any easier. Our vehicles did meet all requirements when being received at the port of entry at Bremerhaven.

Being in Bremerhaven stirred boyhood memories. I had remembered that name well. It was the home base for the U-Boats that plagued the Allied ships in W.W.11. I did manage to visit some old anti-aircraft gun bunkers that still existed in the surrounding countryside. After the acceptance by all bureaucratic officials, these ten units were delivered to ten German cities, ranging from Hamburg in the north to Munich in the south. We had committed to providing a Grumman Olson technician to monitor these units during this evaluation. He would be accompanied by a willing technician provided by G.M. of Europe, located in Russelsheim. I managed a complete tour of all ten of those cities and facilities after the units had been placed into daily service. While thinking my geographic knowledge of Germany was adequate, I had no idea just how varied those different regions were. We were provided with a car from G.M. Europe and had no difficulty traveling around that beautiful country. Having grown up in W.W.11, I had looked at Germans as the enemy. It was a pleasure to now be working daily with these Germans while touring that vast, diverse country. We did discover that Scotch Whisky was expensive in the hotel bars. It could, however, be purchased reasonably at the fuel service stations along our routes. Each vehicle fuel fill would include a bottle of Scotch. The expensive Scotch caused my return to drinking beer and lots of it. Probably adding to my increased body weight, requiring more new clothes. While still evaluating the vehicles submitted by a total of eight potential bidders, the Bundespost announced a significant change in the new vehicle specifications. A new law restricting vehicle size allowed in inner cities was anticipated.

Current large bodies being evaluated would be excluded from future inner-city delivery. A specification for the smaller sized delivery truck of the future was now released.

Each of the manufacturers would be required to submit one new vehicle demonstrating compliance with this new specification. They would continue to use the larger units for evaluation. We now had to rush the production and delivery of a smaller body with different chassis Gross Vehicle Weight Rating, and shorter wheelbase. This new and much smaller body configuration included many similar features. The small truck we presented was well received and met all requirements. We did maintain possession of this unit in Germany. We were instructed to drive this smaller unit to the ten different locations participating in the evaluation for their review. The Grumman Olson technician would use that new prototype for transportation, as he monitored the original ten large units located across Germany. I did join him as we traveled across Germany from north to south. I was still drinking a lot, and that German beer was adding to my excessive body weight. I drank plenty of their various beers on my travels. Drinking beer and driving on the high-speed Autobahn was done as a daily routine. Only drinking Scotch in our hotel rooms in the evening.

Ten of the original Bundesposte larger trucks were located in ten different cities in Germany, from north to south. The smaller vehicle had complied with the new specifications for production units. It was driven to the same ten cities for review. It appeared to be the leading candidate, appearing superior to the other competitor's vehicles submitted for evaluation

Chapter 29 - Travelling in Early Abstinence -

It was during this challenging period of working in Germany that I made that memorable trip to Hazelden in November 1993. My introduction to A.A. and subsequent abstinence from alcohol being initiated in December 1993. Now in February 1994, I would make my first trip back to Germany to check on the ten Bundespost evaluation units. A new daily task would involve locating an English-speaking meeting of Alcoholics Anonymous. I rarely failed to find an English-Speaking A.A. meeting in the cities we visited. On a few occasions, I did attend regular German A.A. meetings. While I did not understand all that was said in German, someone would be willing to translate. Some have described it as ***"The Language of the Heart."*** In addition to working with the Bundespost, I was also working with body-builders and chassis builders to set up production of Grumman Olson Bodies in Germany. We had captured the interest of many as a result of this Bundespost evaluation process. There was obvious market potential for our product in Germany. These days of abstinence endured while traveling can never really be described. I have often stated that ***"Abstinence Sucks."*** I am aware that the rewards did finally materialize, and I was certainly assisted by many during those trying times. The normal workday was not as difficult as I was always busy. At the end of the workday, my associates would proceed to find a nice restaurant. Usually, they would eat but always drink. I was now heading to the hotel to change clothes and find an A.A. meeting somewhere nearby. It was usual that I was the newcomer at these meetings. Then we would have the meeting after the meeting, and I made it through one more day. I was still not sleeping, and my head was in a turmoil. On more than one occasion, I did contemplate taking a flight back to Minnesota to start all over again. Then my ego and pride kicked in, and I hated to admit failure, so I would white knuckle it until my next A.A. meeting. In a very few months, I was exposed to a great variety of different people of different cultures and backgrounds at a variety of A.A. meetings. My pride prohibited me from reaching out for help, but someone always seemed to be there to extend that hand of A.A. All I had to do was suit-up and show-up. I was constantly offered and provided with help regardless of Eddie. My life was beginning to have improvement with less anxiety. I was getting better, maybe not even willing to admit it. Overcoming my skepticism and cynicism would take time. I would realize I had not thought of taking a drink all day until I was heading to the A.A. meeting. Sharing with others in the daily meetings was becoming more honest. I still had a long way to travel, but I was on a good path. These months of early recovery and abstinence were hectic and challenging with extensive travels. It was fortunate that I had a great staff of engineers taking care of all the daily tasks demanded of the truck body business in Michigan. We were also working with General Motors of Mexico to potentially assemble bodies in Mexico for mounting on G.M. chassis produced there. The potential end-user was the largest bakery in that country called Bimbo Baking. They were also entering the U.S. market, taking over some domestic bakeries. I was able to attend the English-Speaking A.A. meetings in Mexico City, which seemed populated by Americans employed in the oil field industry. Business discussions were also ongoing with General Motors of Latin America, who had a headquarters in Miami. This resulted in trips to Venezuela and Brazil. I always found an A.A. meeting wherever my business would take me. I have no idea what my recovery and acceptance of A.A. may have been with only attendance at the local Michigan A.A. meetings. My exposure to so many different people in so many different locations made an impression. Bill Wilson was right when he described one alcoholic talking with another alcoholic as the ***"Language of the Heart."*** What may be more important in early recovery is one alcoholic listening to another alcoholic. We have no idea how it works, but it works, and it is progressive in a positive manner. While being the dominant participant in the truck evaluation process being conducted by the Bundespost, our real chances of winning the award looked bleak. The German politicians were mandating that future government procurement involve production in East Germany. A new condition for doing business with the Bundespost required locating a production facility in East Germany. Neither Grumman nor GM of Europe were willing to give that investment any consideration. All our great efforts seemed to have been in vain. Other German companies were showing continued interest in our truck bodies. I continued working with a German company called Orten Fahrzeuge before the takeover of Grumman Olson by Northrup. All these many ventures would come to a halt with that change in ownership of Grumman Olson. I had experienced and survived the challenges of traveling in foreign countries as an active alcoholic, and also as an alcoholic in early recovery. During those months of abstinence and early recovery, I did lose much of my excess body weight. My closets were full of all sizes of clothes, so there was no need for new purchases. Two years after entering Hazelden weighing 305 pounds, my body weight was approximately 180 pounds. That is probably my weight today if I ever felt a need to check. The ongoing daily miracles experienced in this new life of recovery are difficult to explain. Maybe they can only be experienced. I do attempt to share my struggles and experiences with newcomers. Sometimes thinking if I throw enough shit at the wall, some of it will stick. Always feeling a message of hope can be carried and shared with others.

RouteStar being Demonstrated in Germany by Orten Fabrezeuge

Chapter 30 – Farming Life and Contented Sobriety

The days that started in April 1995 were a new way of daily living and thinking. I would continue my regular A.A. meetings all around the area. I began to tackle the numerous and much-needed tasks of fixing the old and neglected farm. So much to do, and sometimes not knowing where to start. My first order of the day was to step outside and holler in my loud voice, **"Good Morning God,"** which surely beats, saying, **"Good God, Its Morning."** I was not in good physical shape for farm-work, knowing I could only improve with time and effort. I had anticipated being called as a consultant at Northrup-Grumman, feeling my expertise and experience would be missed. That new team of managers did not seem to have any need for my services. I would receive many calls from the sales force and many fleet customers, willingly assisting wherever possible. The new Northrup Voight management team did not value any of my input. They had **a *know it all attitude*.** Unfortunately for many of the dedicated long-term employees, this new management team would run a great company into bankruptcy in four years. Quite unbelievable! Not an easy task, but they did succeed.

 Federal charges were pressed against the new president for fraud, embezzlement, etc. He would die before being convicted, but many innocent people had suffered. Fortunately, the Sturgis production facility was purchased quickly by another truck body company. They would continue to produce aluminum truck bodies under the new Morgan Olson name. The other Grumman Olson and LLV facilities were closed. I never followed up with what happened to those facilities, or the many loyal employees. This new farming life was full of daily challenges that I willingly accepted. A first task was to have a new pole barn built as a combination sheep plus storage barn and garage. Demolishing the two old buildings and putting a new pole barn structure in that same location. New tractor and other implements were needed, and expensive. Additional finances were necessary. I would accept an offer as a consultant engineer for a bus and ambulance manufacturing company in

Elkhart, Indiana. Being only a 40 miles drive and not requiring full-time work proved attractive.

I would supervise the design of new ambulance bodies and rescue trucks. The newly designed ambulance body resulted in a substantial order for the City of Chicago ambulances. The financial compensation was appreciated, but I was always in a quandary about how much time I could neglect the farm. Other consulting tasks involving product liability were also financially rewarding. I did refuse many offers, allowing more time for farming and recovery. Old fences were removed, and fencerows cleared. Pastures fenced and reseeded. Costly and labor-intensive tasks as the farm underwent restoration. This also would provide me with a different thought process and peace of mind. My young friend Rick that I had known for so many years suggested I join him as an A.A. volunteer at the State Prison. He then arranged to have me join him weekly as a guest at the Michigan State prison in Coldwater. I joined him weekly as a guest in February and March of 1996. By April of 1996, I had undergone all the indoctrination required to become an official Michigan Department of Corrections Volunteer. I still do continue as a volunteer with those weekly prison meetings, missing on rare occasions only when circumstances beyond my control prevent my attendance. These meetings are the most favored A.A. meetings I currently participate in each week. Who would have guessed that Eddie Mackay would enjoy going to jail and prison each week? **God has a strange sense of humor!** Although having experience in Scotland and the Catskills with dairy cattle, I had no experience in managing beef cattle. Willing to learn, I soon discovered that handling of Highland Cattle required accommodating the large horns. I proceeded to make my handling area, with a homemade alleyway and chute, utilizing a Foremost 30 head-gate. It all seemed to work quite well for the routine vaccinations when I solicited much-needed help from my friend Rick. He had lots of beef cattle know-how. Rick also had plenty of experience in showing cattle, but Highlands was also something new to him. He had convinced me to enter three animals in the Highland Show at the National Western Stock Show in Denver being held in January 1998. Late in 1997, I had purchased the western five acres plot that had been part of the original homestead. It had been owned by a retired couple for some years and included a nice barn with a mobile home. With the death of the old woman, I negotiated the purchase, adding much-needed acreage. We were able to use the nice barn immediately to prepare the animals for the stock show. Halter training Highlands was a new experience, and I was a willing student. I had purchased a new pick-up truck in 1995 for farm use. We used my truck and Rick`s livestock trailer, heading on the 1200 miles trip to Denver in the January winter weather. Quite an experience for someone who had never driven a truck and trailer. Traversing Michigan, Illinois, Iowa, Nebraska, and Colorado in January may not be the smartest decision. We made it safely with some scary moments. Thank goodness for two good sober drivers, even if one had no truck and trailer experience. That same trip would become an annual event for both of us. I was to miss the trip in 2019 due to health problems, but my able crew maintained the Dundonald Highlands presence at that Highland Show and Sale in Denver. Showing the cattle that year in Denver was my first showing of cattle since 1947 at the local Dundonald Show, as a wee boy in Scotland. *You can take the boy off the farm, but you can`t take the farmer out of the boy.* The show was quite an event, and I sold the heifer calf to a breeder in Washington State and acquired a great new friend. The bull calf entered in the sale was purchased by a breeder in Wisconsin, and we delivered it there with a detour on our journey home. That black bred heifer taken to that show was to become one of my finest brood cows for many years, and her progeny continue to dominate the Dundonald Fold. After the removal of the mobile home from that western portion of the farm, I proceeded to have a nice large pole barn built on that location. This would provide for hay and machinery storage. With already having a well and septic system available, I proceeded to build a nice room in the corner of that pole barn. I named it *"The Bothy."* Most of the horse stables in Scotland had a *Bothy* to accommodate the hired hand. I had spent plenty of time in the Newfield **Bothy**. I was now required to learn basic skills to add plumbing and electric for the kitchen, bathroom, heating, and interior paneling to be added, along with a tiled floor. This made a nice place to have when working with animals at the west barn in winter weather. I also added another chute and head-gate at that west barn for routine cattle chores. A busy farm life with ongoing recovery and so many blessings. With involvement in the American Highland Cattle Association and the regional association, many new friends were being discovered. Combining these friends, along with the many acquaintances from the recovery community, provided an entirely new way of life. While brand new in the farming and recovery life in 1995, it was suggested that I attend the 60th Anniversary International Convention of Alcoholics Anonymous. It was being held in San Diego. Having lots of Frequent Flyer Miles available, I followed that suggestion. *Quite an event for a newbie like me!* Being one of 56,000 sober drunks in the Jack Murphy Stadium reciting the Serenity Prayer was truly a spiritual experience. It removed any left-over skepticism I may have had. While in San Diego, I met a bunch of fellows in A.A. from Ireland. They would convince me to join them in Killarney in 1996, to celebrate 50 years of A.A. in Ireland. I certainly would attend that event, enjoying another great boost to my recovery. That event in Ireland was quite special, and I continue to keep in touch with two women from Dublin and Switzerland that I met while in Killarney. Leaving Killarney, I visited Dublin, also attending an A.A. meeting. Then I headed north to Cookstown County Tyrone, where I had plenty of relatives. Traveling on to Scotland, where I visited with many Highland Cattle Breeders. I became a member of The Highland Cattle Society. Highland Cattle might be just as addictive as Johnnie Walker! Visiting the Highland cattle breeders caused me to visit many remote areas of Scotland. I was always able to find my daily A.A. meeting. With attendance at so many A.A. meetings in

Scotland, I was encouraged to return in 1997 for The Blue Bonnets Gathering of A.A. in Dumfries in Scotland.

Killarney, Ireland - 1996, and Dumfries, Scotland - 1997

This annual Blue Bonnets Gathering held in October allowed for a trip combining this gathering with the Highland Cattle Sale in Oban, also held in October. Attending a regular A.A. meeting while in Oban was a great experience. Some attendees traveled long distances by train and bus to participate in that meeting. I was also able to return to that Oban A.A. meeting in 2005 and 2010 while attending the Oban Highland Cattle Sale. There was always someone who remembered me, and still a meeting after the meeting. That unique *Fellowship of A.A.* is something that can indeed be experienced, but it is difficult to describe. Having participated in many A.A. meetings in my engineering travels, I now enjoy numerous meetings as I travel on my farming business. Attending the A.A. meeting in Denver during the National Western Stock Show, I have met ranchers from Montana, Idaho, and Wyoming. It is interesting hearing the distances they travel to attend their regular A.A. meetings. The Bi-Centennial year of 2000 was unique, with the A.A. International Convention being held in the twin cities of Minneapolis/Saint Paul. I would attend, along with many Hazelden Alumni. Like the event in San Diego, we had a multitude of A.A members from so many countries gathered in the Metro-dome of

Minneapolis, all reciting the Serenity Prayer.

Indeed a spiritual awakening for many. Being surrounded by such a diversity of individuals living in recovery precipitated reflection on my chronic and progressive alcoholism. I believe the three components to my disease were first, having a genetic propensity. Secondly, my upbringing and environment in that drinking culture of Scotland. Thirdly and most significant was Eddie`s Contribution. Three main components of my new life in recovery are first, the Twelve-Step process of living, as suggested by Alcoholics Anonymous. Secondly, the acceptance of the God of My Experience, and thirdly no doubt Eddie`s Contribution. I do not ever take my gift of sobriety for granted.

There is no free lunch. I do maintain an attitude of gratitude. I do my utmost to be a wee bit spiritual at some time during each day. A significant happening in that Bi-Centennial year was meeting with a fine gentleman named Bill P. at the Tiebout Reunion. Bill P. being initially from the Twin Cities, had traveled to New York City, spending many years as the archivist in A.A. Central Office. He was a student of the history of A.A., having met with many of the early members. He had recently spent a year preparing a presentation of 100 years of alcoholism in America. Documenting the many treatments attempted between 1900 and 2000. We enjoyed a condensed version of that presentation. This set off a trigger in my head, prompting my extensive reading of those early days of A.A. with only 100 members being involved in the first four years. I became hooked on the history of Alcoholics Anonymous. I am still amazed that this simple solution can work so well when so many other trials and experiments have failed.

Using the term simple, I mean it is not complicated. I do not say easy, as I know it is not easy, but it does get easier. One favorite book by Bill P. is called *"Drop the Rock."* This book provides much-needed assistance for newcomers attempting Steps Six and Seven. I listened to Bill speak on the original *"Mary Drop the Rock."* and also the talk by Sandy B. called *"Drop the Rock."* Like much passed along in A.A., we rarely know the origins, and that is of little importance. I do like to provide a copy of this book after listening to a Fifth Step with any newcomer.

Chapter 31 - Farming and Conservation -

In 1999 I had the opportunity to purchase fifteen acres on the east side of my existing farm. This acreage provided additional grazing for the expanding sheep and Highland cattle folds. My retired neighbor owned a beautiful home with 28 acres and decided to sell. I only wanted the grazeable portion, but he refused to divide the property. I went ahead and purchased everything, with the idea of dividing the property and selling the home with 13 acres quickly. Not as easy as anticipated, taking a year to shed that high-cost impulsive purchase. A stressful venture with all turning out well. This property also had the river running through, and I have always been fascinated by waterways. I had never imagined owning such a beautiful small farm with the Prairie River running across the southern portion. The Highland cattle also loved that river with a good gravel bottom. Cows would stand up to their belly`s in water, before moving to a hillside to allow the breeze to cool them off in our hot summer days. Unfortunately, many canoeists also traveled that same river and were frightened by Highland cattle standing in the river. The State of Michigan received complaints, resulting in my being notified to fence the animals away from the river.
This was not a practical idea with the river running through flood-plain, swamp, and wooded areas. Maintenance of such a fence would be cost-prohibitive. I proceeded to have discussions with local Conservation personnel as to how best to demonstrate compliance with the State of Michigan Mandate. Together we reviewed many suggested ideas with most being impractical or too costly. I then engineered my satisfactory solution. A new fence was installed at the cleared portion where the cattle frequently entered the river. We then added a natural barrier using fallen trees and limbs on the less open areas of the riverbank. A lovely new pond was excavated adjacent to the favored watering area of the river,

with a gentle driveway style approach, including black cloth covered with small stones. A fence across the pond limited the access to prevent the cattle from turning it into a mudhole. This lovely pond was equipped with two aerators, and as I surmised, it maintained the same water level as the river. The cattle could continue to now stand up to their belly's in the pond, although the whole herd could not do this simultaneously.

Highland cattle have an established pecking order, and this is where it can be observed. This effort was well received by the Conservation Office in the county. They documented my initiatives, allowing this information to be provided to other livestock owners with river-lands. I was also convinced to give some time as a member of the Conservation Board of Saint Joseph County. I did act as a board member for many years. During my time with this conservation board, I became aware of the new Michigan Agriculture Environmental Program. This program was established to provide guidelines for maintaining a quality environment. I was attracted to be part of this effort. I liked the fact that participation was voluntary and not mandated.

When Dundonald Farm became MAEAP verified in 2008, it was only for Farmstead System, since the verification for Livestock Systems had only been set up for large livestock operations. I began working with various interested individuals to have guidelines prepared for small livestock systems, such as I operated. Dundonald Farm would then become the first farm to be MAEAP verified for this new Livestock System in 2010. Although doing minimal crop farming, Dundonald Farm is currently MAEAP verified for Farmstead System, Livestock System, and Crop System, continuing to maintain a healthy environment. Having farmers do the right things voluntarily achieves much better results than having bureaucrats mandate rules for farmers. I have been blessed to have the opportunity to be a good steward of the environment in one wee corner of Michigan. The farming of sheep and Highland cattle proved to be just what I needed for a new way of life in Recovery

.Having always believed whatever you do, do well, that carried into my breeding of quality Highland cattle. The American Highland Cattle breeders initiated Bull Testing Programs in 1999, and I was an eager participant. The positive performance results of all the bulls I entered was encouraging, and I felt I was on the right track. Bull tests would continue through 2006, Dundonald Highland's bulls always proving to be of top quality. Maybe I got lucky when making my initial purchases of Highlands. While many of my original animals had excellent pedigrees and conformation, their disposition left much to be desired. With having a good cowman in my friend Rick, the disposition of the Highlands in Dundonald Fold became a priority and is evident here today. Having gentle cows leads to having gentle calves, making life more pleasurable for the caretakers.

Life was going exceptionally well until I was diagnosed with rectal cancer in 2004, with surgery recommended. Returning home from this depressing diagnosis with my daughter driving, I instructed her to stop at the party store to allow my purchase of a bottle of Johnnie Walker. I have no idea what precipitated that thought. It just seemed the thing to do. She merely said she would drop me off at home, having something to attend to, and would return later to take me to the liquor store, if I needed the Scotch. Back at home, feeling weird and confused, I immediately contacted a Tiebout friend in Toronto. I was aware he was involved in the A.A. International Convention being planned there in 2005. I requested he give me information on a nice hotel outside the inner city since I wanted to make an early reservation for that convention. The hotel clerk thought I was crazy, making a reservation more than a year ahead. She did take my information along with a deposit, and my plans were made for Toronto in 2005. I never did purchase the Johnnie Walker, nor have I ever considered such action since that day. Crazy thoughts from who knows where, protected with no fuss, by a loving stepdaughter. With my rectum removed, due to cancer, this Scotsman is no longer a complete asshole.

MEAEP Verification June 2010 — Highlands In Prairie River

Chapter 32 - Continue – Continue – Continue -

Getting involved in the showing of Highland cattle, it became evident that I needed a show-box, divider panels, and grooming chute. These items were expensive to purchase. With my knowledge of aluminum fabrication, and having sources for aluminum sheet and extrusions, I proceeded to fabricate my own. It was evident there was a potential market available for such livestock show products. I felt I could also improve the features of the products currently available. My new aluminum fabrication business was started, providing some additional income. My finished garage was quickly converted into a fabrication shop. I then proceeded to advertise my aluminum show products. I had a willingness to produce custom products, and there appeared a market for products to accommodate the horns of the Highlands. Today I continue to provide aluminum fabricated products upon request due to my lack of energy required. I do still enjoy doing some limited aluminum fabrication. Producing high-quality products from aluminum sheet and extrusions with solid rivets provides personal satisfaction.

After a successful showing in the Stock Show in Denver in 1998, we decided to enter some Highlands in our local Saint Joseph County Fair here in Centreville. Since they had no Highland Cattle Class, we had to show with the All Other Breeds, but it was a start to another venture. The Fair Board would create a class for Highlands for the following year, and we had a great turnout of Highlands from all over the Midwest Region. That event is still one of six Highland Shows that we participate in annually. The location is close to the farm and takes a whole week in September. I can usually meet up with many of my old engineering associates during that week. It provides an opportunity to revisit my old way of life with so many people that had assisted me along my journey.

Saint Joseph County Grange Fair, Centreville Michigan

Having survived rectal cancer in 2004 was a blessing with my sister and brother in law coming from Canada to maintain the farm and livestock operation. Both being retired, my brother in law had plenty of farm experience. I requested that they return again in 2005 to permit me another visit to Scotland. After the cancer scare, that trip seemed needed. This was a great trip, allowing me to travel around and visit many Highland Folds. No matter where my travel took me, I would attend the local A.A. meetings. I had already made that great trip to Toronto in 2005 for the International Convention of Alcoholics Anonymous. Having spent many occasions on business in Toronto with the usual excessive drinking, this sober visit was unique. So many diverse people from across the globe have discovered a common solution to that common problem. The Toronto gathering being my third such event, I know I have been blessed, despite my previous destructive lifestyle. My activities with the American Highland Cattle Association and the Midwest Highland Cattle Association have involved being a director and president of both. I have always done my utmost to encourage and support Junior members of both organizations. They will hopefully be the future caretakers of The Grande Olde Breed. The year 2006 provided an opportunity to purchase additional acreage directly across the road from my farm. I had been grazing this land, and now I owned it. Having now expanded the originally purchased farm to the west, the east, and the north. Not much possibility of any future expansion in this county where farmland is at a premium. I will just be satisfied with my small corner in southwest Michigan.

Nowadays, we do participate in six Highland shows annually. I usually prefer having some of the younger generations do the actual showing. My friend Rick does all the grooming, I relax and enjoy. When previously showing my cattle, I always wore one of the five Mackay tartan kilts, being a traditionalist in many ways. On one occasion, a rambunctious young bull being shown at the Denver Stock Show managed to somehow flip me over in the show-ring. The audience was entertained, and they no longer need to ask that stupid question about what the Scotsman wears under his kilt? I am well remembered even if that young bull was mediocre.

The American Highland Cattle Association played host to the International Convention of Highland Cattle Breeders in Wyoming in 2006. This was quite a gathering, meeting with foreign breeders. I already knew many from being at Oban Sales in Scotland through the years. Also meeting more new friends from the U.S., Canada, and overseas. I found myself at ease when joining in the night-life activities, where plenty of alcohol was consumed, never feeling tempted to indulge. *I came a long way, baby!* The expanded farming operation and the lifestyle I had adopted was both healthy and rewarding. In addition to our six Highland shows, we regularly participate in the Michigan State Beef Expo, with a display of Highlands. I joined the Michigan Cattleman's Association but limited my involvement to one springtime event. The increased number of cattle and sheep on the small acreage dictated the purchase of all winter feed supplies and supplemental feed to compliment the excellent quality rotational grazing. To provide good quality grazing in the dry summer months, I had installed a K-Line pod irrigation system. This being done in two phases, it involved significant expense. Irrigation is hugely beneficial during our periods of limited rainfall. Farm income is insufficient to cover ongoing farm expenses proves to be a constant problem. Tapping into previous stock investments and savings is an annual necessity. Hopefully, with a wee bit of luck and some ingenuity, we can continue our charming lifestyle for many more years. The aging process with reduced energy levels has limited fabrication efforts. Maybe just getting lazy, needing a kick in the butt!

Highland Cattle Society did host another International Convention in Scotland in 2010, and that was a pleasurable trip. Visiting Highland breeder friends, A.A. friends, and my remaining relatives kept me busy. I do hope to be able to make another trip back to Scotland in the future years. I do enjoy a good life on the farm, with continued involvement in A.A. events, including jail and prison meetings, also having peace of mind. Hazelden would humble me with the inclusion of my story of *"Kilts, Cows, and Usefulness"* in the Spring 2014 issue of **"The Voice"** publication. A photographer from Kalamazoo spent a sunny winter morning here on the farm. I spoke at length with the nice woman doing the writing of my story of farming and living in Recovery.

The American Highland Cattle Association Annual Convention provides an excellent opportunity for breeders from across the country to gather, visit, and share information and stories. The location varies for these events, which adds to the attraction. While traveling extensively in business, most of what I experienced was hotel rooms and barrooms. Nowadays, I do take time to enjoy the many interests as I travel. The year 2015 found us, breeders, gathering in northern New England's beautiful scenic area. While being a participant enjoying that convention, I was astonished to be one of two new members selected for the AHCA Hall Of Fame. Yes, a humbling experience, being recognized by my peers for my contributions toward promoting and maintaining The Grande Olde Breed. To think that my original reason for purchasing Highlands was part of my ninth step amends, in memory of Patricia's wishes, and now being recognized as a Highland breeder. Patricia would indeed have been proud of the Dundonald Highlands Fold.

I can smile and say, **"Thank You, Dear God." In** January 2016, after numerous tests, I was diagnosed with Penile cancer, with immediate surgery advised. This aggressive cancer would require me to have a Penectomy. I underwent surgery on March 2nd at the University of Michigan Cancer Center. Never having heard the word Penectomy prior, they just cut off my pecker. I did my best to stay tough. Even requesting, the surgeon place it in a bottle of Johnnie Walker, but he could not be convinced. When asking the reason for my request, I stated that placing the bottle on a shelf, I could observe one old friend of forty years, along with another special friend of eighty years. Both could then be well remembered. He was not convinced. One of my Hazelden friends said, just as well, as I may have drunk it someday. It was a wee bit scary, and I no longer claim to be fearless, but I did survive. I was also able to make it back to Center City, MN, two weeks after surgery, for the Tiebout reunion. Still a smiling Scotsman with another good story to tell. This aggressive cancer then showed up in my Lymph nodes, requiring more surgery. I managed to survive that event also.

I had the inconvenience of drain tubes hanging from my groins for some months. Still not deterred from participation in the Highland shows. Just a crazy Scotsman with drain tubes hanging below my kilt. The Good Lord is keeping me around for some purpose, and I will do my utmost to fulfill whatever that task entails. Being part of the U. of M. Cancer Research group required thorough tests on a six- month interval. With good results observed, that is now an annual event. I have been blessed once more for some unexplainable reason. The importance of attending the annual reunion at Hazelden cannot be easily explained. While on the Tiebout unit, I often heard it said there was magic in those brick walls. I would come to believe that it was true. When the old unit was torn down and those brick walls replaced in 2012, we were fortunate that another believer would save some of these magic bricks. All attendees at the reunion of 2013 would receive one of the memorable bricks. Visitors to my home wonder why I have an old brick prominently displayed, and I smile when explaining that it has some special magic in it.

Just an old Hazelden Brick with Magic —— A Special AHCA Honor

Some may question my return to Hazelden each Reunion. In those early years with George W. and Paul H., I struggled for knowledge and understanding of this new way of life. As I began to live with contented sobriety, it now seems I now had a hunger to find more effective ways to carry the message of hope. Two individuals that I would meet each year would help to open my mind. Fred H., who ran the Lodge Program, and John M. heading spiritual care, were attractions for me. Around them, I was all ears. Both these individuals were quite different, but they had a collective strength in the knowledge of life in recovery. Fred, being very much the scholar, spoke in such great depth of the Big Book, like a college professor. John, with his unusual presentation of spirituality, added some real unique humor. I find that humor can be valuable when working with newcomers. I miss the presence of both those mentors, who are no longer at Hazelden. I will no doubt gravitate to someone new as I continue my annual pilgrimage.

The year 2016 was not my easiest, with the challenges of overcoming my health issues. Fortunately, in having excellent help from my sidekick Rick, the farming was well taken care of. The year of 2017 moved right along with farming and recovery routines being the way of life at Dundonald Farm. Maybe a wee bit slower, but still feeling quite fit. While continuing my weekly prison meetings, I did become aware of an inmate scheduled for a Public Parole Hearing. I was anxious to attend. This was a totally new experience, receiving permission to attend and speak on his behalf. He was an inmate I had known close to ten years in our weekly A.A. meetings. Having witnessed the positive changes in this individual over these years, I had no doubt he deserved to be paroled after many years of incarceration. Fortunately, when successfully released, he would live within our county. Meeting him weekly at local A.A. meetings, it seemed a good idea to have him come and live with me in my old farmhouse where I lived alone. I was shocked when notified by the Michigan State Prison, where I had been a volunteer since 1996, that I was no longer welcome. It was thought my closeness to a parolee made me an undesirable volunteer for weekly A.A. meetings. After a hearing with the warden to discuss my relationship with this parolee, good sense did prevail, and my volunteer status was then reinstated. The joke in prison is that while most people fight to get out of prison, there is a crazy Scotsman who would fight to get into prison. I am privileged to continue with those rewarding weekly meetings in that Michigan State Prison.

Chapter 33 - Health Issues and Bounce Back –

As we prepared for the 23rd annual trip to the Denver Stock Show scheduled in January 2019, I was to experience another health problem. Returning from the weekly prison A.A. meeting on Dec. 26th, I experienced a bellyache, but no big deal. Getting progressively worse during the next day, it became severe enough for Rick to drive me to the Kalamazoo emergency center in the wee hours of Dec. 28th. The diagnosis was a Gall bladder problem, requiring surgery. Surgery was scheduled for Saturday morning, December 29th, and I anticipated being home late Saturday or early Sunday. As I had heard before, **"Shit Happens,"** and recovery did not go well. Either from just bad luck or maybe incompetence, my bowel would be ruptured, requiring additional surgery to fix that problem.

After the second surgery, my system did not get started as anticipated. Eventually, my digestive system was functioning, and I was discharged. Two days later, I was back in the emergency center with a severe abdomen infection, requiring the installation of a drain tube. I was stuck with that drain tube until April of 2019. In addition to the drain tube, I acquired a bacterial infection causing me to miss the National Highland show in Denver in 2019. My good friends Rick and Kolton maintained the Dundonald Highlands presence at that great event. During my stay in that Kalamazoo hospital, I can honestly say I was scared. I do not recall ever having felt afraid of anything, but this was a scary experience. I just felt this was not the way to go, and it seemed that I had too many unfinished tasks needing completion. My various life experiences, good and bad, passed before my eyes as I lay awake in that facility. Maybe I had always taken my good fortunes for granted, feeling invincible. I did manage to bounce back, although it did take until the spring of 2019 before I was any semblance of my usual self. Still able to attend the annual Tiebout reunion in March, and for that, I was grateful. Getting back into aluminum fabrication again as I recovered, it seemed that so many pieces of my fabrication equipment were failing, requiring replacement. My fabrication shop had been set up 22 years ago, so fixing and replacement of some items could be expected. With no longer having the physical strength to do the necessary farm chores, Rick has taken over practically all those daily tasks. I do enjoy still being able to continue with the fabrication of a variety of products, enjoying a good healthy life, while doing my best to be useful to others.

The A.A. jail meetings and prison meetings are still weekly events, along with my homegroup meetings. I do enjoy continuing the monthly meetings of the Saint Joseph County Community Corrections Advisory Board while putting a face on recovery. My body is slowing, but my head keeps working. The longer I am sober, the more I recognize the power of alcoholism and addiction. Maybe as a youngster, I had some flaws, with the alcohol camouflaging those flaws. I do believe alcohol did something for me, and then eventually, it would do a lot more to me. Maybe my excessive drinking was a chemical solution for my spiritual problem. Left to my own resources, I will surely drink, as evidenced by my previous 41 years of drinking. Given my current way of living and thinking each day, I believe the decision to not drink is made for me, and not made by me. Maintaining that daily ***"Attitude of Gratitude"*** is a significant component. I have my understanding of what gratitude is. Gratitude is an admission that we are not self-sufficient, nor do we need to be. We become grateful when we give up attempting to be self-sufficient and can accept help. When we willingly accept help from outside ourselves. I am also convinced my ongoing contented sobriety is directly proportional to my usefulness to others. I do feel that **Peace of Mind is Worth any Chore!**

Chapter 34 - 2020 Another Leap Year -

The year 2020 started off so much better than had the year of 2019. Once more, we would prepare for that westward trip to Denver in January. The National Western Stock Show is an event that I have been privileged to attend on 23 of 24 years. Taking four Dundonald Highlands entries plus five head for Skye High Farm, we had a full livestock trailer. We headed once more on that long 1200 miles trip to Denver. Blessed with clear and cold weather with dry highways made travel smoother—one more Western Stock Show. February began with a beautiful sunny Saturday and a busy lambing season. The month ended on the 29^{th,} being a leap year. It was nice to be blessed with having good health and able to celebrate the 21st anniversary of my birth. Eighteen good friends provided me with a surprise luncheon. Receiving many cards and calls and messages wishing me well from the many people I have met along this journey. The well-wishes from friends from my engineering life and my current farming and recovery life emphasized how fortunate I am to have been so truly blessed.

The annual Tiebout reunion in March 2020 was planned and would have been my 27th Reunion. Due to the Coronavirus 2019 pandemic, this reunion, like so many events, was canceled. I did manage to contact and speak with a few of the close friends that I have always looked forward to meeting at Hazelden. Similarly, the Michigan Cattlemen1s Beef Expo was canceled. The 2020 International Convention Alcoholics Anonymous, Detroit, MI. was also canceled. That location would have been extra special, having drunk so much, and so often in Motown. A troubled time for many with this virus causing the whole country a real slowdown. Isolating on the farm is not a problem, providing our necessary supplies are still available. We are probably more fortunate than many. No weekly jail or prison A.A. meetings, with these facilities all quarantined. I do trust and pray that this critical situation will pass without too many being negatively affected. It does allow people an opportunity to work together for a common cause. There are plenty of new opportunities to be useful in some small way on any given day. This does seem to be an excellent time to wrap up the story of my life in engineering, farming, and recovery. So many blessings as I travel on this path that has been provided. I continue with my attitude of gratitude, giving thanks to the God of My Experience. Now with the completion of this story of a ***"Recovered Alcoholic,"*** I will provide my understanding of what those Twelve Steps of Alcoholics Anonymous mean to me in my daily life. This listing and description are personal and not intended to precipitate debate or opinions—just another blessed experience.

Maybe I will be remembered for something other than Ugly Trucks

One of my favorite parts of "The Big Book" is found at the end of Page 164- ***"We shall be with you in the Fellowship of the Spirit, and you will surely meet some of us as you trudge the Road of Happy Destiny. May God bless you and keep you until then."***

Chapter 35 - The Twelve Steps Process of Living -

<u>12 Steps of Alcoholics Anonymous – How I understand these steps and use them in my daily way of living – Life is but a day at most.</u>
With the 12 steps being part of the book called Alcoholics Anonymous and known as **"The Big Book,"** there have been endless discussions and debates on how to use them or work them. I try to avoid such disputes, although I may be tempted to enlighten some on historical facts. Having them presented to me as guidelines on how to start the process of changing my drinking way of life to a sober life was all that concerned me. I was initially told that these 12

Steps were a group of principles, spiritual in nature, which, if practiced as a way of life, could expel my obsession to drink. I am aware that the early members of A.A. did not use 12 steps, six steps, or any steps, and yet they were blessed with great success. They certainly embodied the principles which are now part of these 12 steps, along with the assumptions of the Oxford Group. The steps I believe are about a way of life, having nothing at all to do with ***not drinking.*** With my cynicism, skepticism, and lack of faith, I indeed needed specific steps, guidelines, and mentors to get me on the right path. I have also looked back to the writings by and about The Oxford Group, believing their influence could undoubtedly be credited with A.A`s existence. I do think the ***Fellowship of A.A.*** has everything to do with ***not drinking.*** My notes on the various steps are strictly personal and not intended to be a challenge as to what others may think or believe. I also quite willingly accept the principles associated with each step. I understand these principles to be - Step 1 - Honesty, Step 2 - Hope, Step 3 - Faith, Step 4 - Courage, Step 5- Integrity, Step 6 – Willingness, Step 7 – Humility, Step 8 – Compassion, Step 9 – Justice, Step 10 – Perseverance, Step 11 – Spiritual Awareness, and Step 12 – Service.

While I may not always adhere to these principles in my daily life, I do make an effort to be a wee bit spiritual at some time throughout each day. Each day begins with an attitude of gratitude. My morning prayer is often just asking God to keep his arm around my shoulder and his hand over my mouth. My friend George W. suggested that I never miss an opportunity to just shut up. When working with newcomers, I try not to dictate my interpretations of these steps. I do insist on having them read from both the Big Book and the Twelve Steps and Twelve Traditions, just as I was instructed. It worked for me and should work for anyone with the willingness to accept the ***Twelve Steps way of life,*** as suggested as a program of recovery from that hopeless state of mind and body. The Twelve Step program embraces living itself, and practicing these steps allows us to no longer be prisoners of addiction with its many negatives.

STEP ONE – *"We admitted we were powerless over alcohol – that our lives had become unmanageable."*

I do believe this first step is our problem statement. Lack of power and unmanageability. These two problems are intertwined, and it is difficult for many to accept both simultaneously. I willingly accepted my lack of power over Johnnie Walker Whisky. I was initially reluctant to admit that my life was unmanageable. I would concede to my innermost self that I was an alcoholic. That was my first step in recovery. I functioned at a high level in engineering management and avoided severe legal problems. I still thought I was managing my life quite well. It took some discussions to make me aware that I was managing my alcoholism. That had become a full-time job. My lack of power and resultant unmanageability, being then admitted to and accepted entirely. Not liking the term surrender, until informed that I needed to surrender to win. This seemed like a contradiction, but I was willing to try. When working with newcomers today, I suggest that they need to Admit, Accept, and Adjust. It is not easy- but it does get easier. I marvel how our co-founders arrived at this ***First Step.*** It was difficult for someone with my ego and arrogant attitude to accept the hopelessness of my condition with the progression of my alcoholism.

STEP TWO - *"Came to believe that a power greater than ourselves could restore us to sanity."*

Accepting that Step One is the problem, then Step Two could undoubtedly be our solution. Easy two-step program. Well, maybe not so easy. While aware that I was not clinically insane, I could accept that my previous destructive way of life exhibited irrational and crazy behavior. I did have a desire to eliminate the negative consequences of my excessive drinking. It was easy to accept my lack of power. My difficulty was accepting that some force or vague God would eliminate the desire to drink. I would never doubt there was a God. I had worn the feathers of the Angels wings, with the numerous events leading to my nickname of ***"Crash Mackay."*** I was raised in the Church of Scotland, with Sunday School, Bible

Classes, Communion, and regular attendance. After leaving Scotland, I drifted away from any participation in any church events. The caring Chaplain suggested I go ahead and take this second step with blind faith, being sure I would *"come to believe,"* when willing to make a sincere effort. We cannot turn on a belief, hence *"Came to Believe."* He also said that listening to the sober members of A.A. would be helpful if I had an open mind. I did have some reluctant willingness to believe. That would eventually become real willingness. Today that *"power greater than myself"* is never in question. I have experienced so many blessings along this path that I travel. For myself, that power has become the *God of my Experience*, and I do believe that I am a *"Child of God,"* and *God is Good*. I do my utmost to be a wee bit spiritual at some time of each day. I do attempt to make a conscious effort to be useful to others.

STEP THREE – "Made a decision to turn our will and our lives over to the care of God as we understood him"

With the acceptance of Step One as my problem, and somewhat hesitantly believing Step Two to be my solution, I was now ready to address Step Three. Although initially addressing this step as a scholar, it took some discussions to convince me what was really needed. My major obstacles being my willpower and perceived intelligence. I did accept that I would be making a willing decision to make the necessary changes in my way of life. I also understood that I would still be accountable for my behavior and all of my actions. Different people provided me with useful insights. It was suggested that I try each day to follow *God's Will, not My Will.* I also used the Third Step Prayer. *"God, I offer myself to Thee – To build with me and to do with me as thou wilt. Relieve me of the bondage of self, that I may better do Thy Will. Take away my difficulties, that victory over them may bear witness to those I would help of Thy Power, Thy Love, and Thy Way of life. May I do Thy will always"!* I made the decision to do my best by turning it over, now being prepared to move on to the Fourth Step.

When working with newcomers today, I suggest they make the

decision to change and then get out of the way. I may also inform them that willpower has been proven worthless when it comes to stopping an alcoholic from taking a drink. To those in doubt, I suggest they gag down a box of EX-Lax and try using their willpower to stop taking a shit.

STEP FOUR – "*Made a searching and fearless moral inventory of ourselves."*

While having no idea what this inventory process would entail, it did seem a logical step. Having made that decision to change when taking Step-Three, I now had to know what I needed to change. I did not have a clue while living in delusion. I proceeded to get involved in daily discussions with both counselor and Chaplain. I was still having difficulty with my inventory listing. At least my efforts were genuine. After making my final presentation as required for my Fifth Step, the Chaplain did provide real encouragement for my future endeavors. After close to a year of abstinence, and with the guidance of Mark and Joe at the A.A. Big Book Workshop, my fourth attempt at this personal inventory was quite comprehensive. I am convinced the direction in the Big Book Page 65 is helpful by using the three columns. I do recommend adding a fourth column with a heading of - My Contribution. This idea comes from the Big Book Page 67, where the paragraph starts with – *Referring to our list again. Putting out of our minds the wrongs others had done, we resolutely looked at our own mistakes.* Accepting my contribution had me acting like a mature adult, and it was about time. George W. had emphasized that recovery was for grown-ups. Today when making decisions, I often ask, *"What would a mature adult do"?.* This Fourth Step requires assistance and encouragement from a good sponsor or mentor. One does need to be careful; they are not overwhelmed by past actions. *"We will not regret the past nor wish to shut the door on it,"* is an excellent ninth step promise. I am aware of some members who repeat the fourth step at regular intervals. I have not subscribed to that practice. Living the Tenth Step daily in a thorough manner eliminates my personal need to return to the fourth step. Many buried items did surface later, and those were addressed as expeditiously as possible.

STEP FIVE – **_"Admitted to God, to ourselves, and to another human being, the exact nature of our wrongs."_**

No doubt, this is an ego deflation step. As was pointed out early, my arrogance, ego, and lack of humility were major obstacles I needed to overcome. Even accepting that as a necessity, it still requires an ongoing conscious effort. It has been said often – my ego could be deflated today and be riding horseback tomorrow. The biggest problem initially with this step was my belief that some wrongs I would take to my grave. Today I may even joke about some of those things, although indeed not proud of many of my actions. Knowing my God was already aware of my actions, having to share these things with another human being was a real problem. I did find myself sharing different things with different people. My sponsor told me of someone just like me, who took a Chinaman not understanding English, out on Lake Michigan on his boat to do his Fifth Step. Not needing to go that far, I would eventually do this step entirely with a fine priest, also in the fellowship of A.A. It did feel good. Even if I had to pocket my pride. This happened in my second year of abstinence. Today I love to emphasize the 5th step promises when working with newcomers. *Once we have taken this step, withholding nothing, we are delighted. We can look the world in the eye. We can be alone at perfect peace and ease. Our fears fall from us. We begin to feel the nearness of our creator. We may have had certain spiritual beliefs, but now we begin to have a spiritual experience. The feeling that the drink problem has disappeared will often come strongly. We feel we are on the Broad Highway, walking hand in hand with the Spirit of the Universe.*

STEP SIX – **_"Were entirely ready to have God remove all these defects of character."_**

This is the step separating the men from the boys, as quoted in the Twelve Steps and Twelve Traditions. It is also often stated that with this step, willingness is the key. Like many others, I no doubt initially gave this step lip service. There had been no eagerness to admit to or recognize that I had real character defects. Addressing some possible character defects, I had ignored the most severe defects being Lack of humility and Ego. Even although my lack of humility, ego, and arrogance was continually pointed out by many. While doing so much better after the Big Book Workshop, I really feel the best tool for Steps Six and Seven is the book by Hazelden called **"Drop the Rock."** I had been privileged to listen to the author Bill P. speak on many occasions. It felt good to hear Bill speak on **"Drop the Rock"** as a topic before the publication of this book. I have provided copies of this book to many newcomers after doing a fifth step. I also recommend the follow-up book – ***"Drop the Rock – The Ripple Effect."*** A Hazelden publication by Fred H. It allows using Step Ten daily to practice steps six and seven. I do use and recommend this *"Usefulness prayer."*

God, help me today to find balance between my character defects and the Principles of the Program. So as to be useful, to myself, all others, and you, The God of my Experience.

<u>STEP SEVEN – "Humbly asked Him to remove our shortcomings."</u>

The key ingredient in this step is humility. This reference to my lack of humility had been evident to many as my major problem. As sung by Mac Davis and Willie Nelson, ***"Oh Lord It`s Hard to Be Humble,"*** This certainly applied to me. That cocky attitude was part of me even as a kid. I do believe the arrogance had followed later in my life. I did research so many definitions of humility while struggling with this obvious flaw. One description was that ***"humility is the ability to learn from others."*** With reflection on my earlier life, I knew I had been a good student. In my younger years, I must have had humility. Likewise, I was eager to learn the automotive business from anyone willing to share their knowledge. That lack of humility and my arrogant attitude had somehow just slipped into my persona. Maybe it was a defense with the progression of my alcoholism. I willingly decided that I would humbly accept guidance from others in this new venture of attempting sobriety. That guidance was voluntarily being provided from members of the fellowship of Alcoholics Anonymous. My new-found pursuit of knowledge of the Big Book of Alcoholics Anonymous and its origins became one of my many blessings. Humility would become what I wanted my attitude to be. I may still not always succeed, but I do have awareness. I do like the Seventh Step prayer –

"My Creator, I am now willing that you should have all of me, good and bad. I pray that you now remove from me every single defect of character which stands in the way of my usefulness to you and my fellows. Grant me strength, as I go out from here, to do your bidding. Amen".

STEP EIGHT – *"Made a list of all persons we had harmed, and became willing to make amends to them all."*

Addressing this step in my first effort, I was hardly aware of just how many people I had harmed in my many years of reckless living. Fortunately, I was guided in my efforts by many members of A.A. I would also seek assistance from the Tiebout Chaplain when returning to Hazelden for the reunions. I was clearly instructed to only concentrate on Step Eight. I had initially been thinking ahead to Step Nine and wondering how I could ever make amends. This proved to be good advice for me. Removing my judgmentalism to the best of my ability did allow a decent effort with my willingness to make a complete list. Other items and past actions would frequently pop into my mind much later. Those were addressed immediately and never would to be buried again. My listing did include some anonymous individuals that had been exposed to an arrogant, egotistical alcoholic in a management position. My new life would hopefully avoid repeating that behavior. Many others were individuals that were no longer with us, and they were added to my extensive list.

STEP NINE – *"Made direct amends to such people wherever possible, except when to do so would injure them or others."*

Having a comprehensive Step Eight listing, I did not rush into the amends process. I did spend time discussing how best to accomplish this with many A.A. members that I felt comfortable with. Some obvious amends had been made immediately with family members, and others close to me. Making amends to those who had passed on created a challenge. I developed some creative ideas which eventually provided me with peace of mind. I would also discover in the business world, that many individuals were unaware of my past behavior being objectionable, thinking it was just "MACKAY." I do not subscribe to saying I am sorry, since we have no credibility. Explaining how I felt I had wronged, and then saying, *"what can I do to make it right"?* That seemed to make more sense to me. I am convinced that my ongoing daily way of living allows me to make continuous amends for my previous destructive lifestyle.

STEP TEN – *"Continued to take personal inventory and when we were wrong promptly admitted it."*

Having worked my way through the previous nine steps with help from many sources, I was comfortable with addressing Step Ten. As told to me by a good friend, having my side of the street clean, I needed to keep it that way. It did take some time to be aware of that word *"promptly,"* and I can smile since it seems to be specifically directed at me. Being an expert at procrastination, this idea of *"promptly admitting"* caused me to smile inwardly on many occasions. Never liking to admit to ever being wrong, I tried doing a better job at being right. There are some promises in this step that may take time to absorb and accept, as even being possible. *We have entered the world of the Spirit. We have ceased fighting anything or anyone - even alcohol. For by this time, sanity will have returned. We will seldom be interested in liquor, if tempted, we recoil from it as from a hot flame. We act sanely and normally, and we find this has happened automatically. We will see that our new attitude toward liquor has been given us without any thought or effort on our part. It just comes! That is the miracle of it. We are not fighting it, neither are we avoiding temptation. We feel we*

have been placed in a position of neutrality – safe and protected. We have not even sworn off. Instead, the problem has been removed. It does not exist for us. We are neither cocky nor are we afraid. That is our experience. These unbelievable promises are followed by a vital warning which states – *That is how we react so long as we keep in a fit spiritual condition.* Having accepted Step Ten to be an integral part of my daily routine of living, I strived to find how to keep in a fit spiritual condition. That continues to be an ongoing challenge. I will never take my sobriety for granted. Initially, I did struggle with the part where step ten says – *"Love and tolerance of others is our code"* since tolerance was not one of my strengths. After a suggestion that I should become less judgmental, then tolerance became easier. I do continue each day to act like a decent human being. I Continue trying to be useful in some way to someone. It is really nice to be useful anonymously. Seeking constant guidance from the **"God of My Experience."**
<u>**STEP ELEVEN** – *"Sought through prayer and meditation to improve our conscious contact with God as we understood Him, praying only for his will and the power to carry it out."*</u>
This Eleventh Step maybe was easier for me as a result of my first meeting with George Weller. With only three months of abstinence, and certainly not feeling good about my new life, George assigned me the task of reading page 86 of the Big Book. I was instructed to begin with the paragraph – *When we retire at night, we constructively review our day. Were we resentful, selfish, dishonest, or afraid? Have we kept something to ourselves which should be discussed with another person at once? Were we kind and loving toward all? What could we have done better? Were we thinking of ourselves most of the time? Or were we thinking of what we could do for others, of what we could pack into the stream of life? But we must be careful not to drift into worry, remorse, or morbid reflection. For that would diminish our usefulness to others. After making our review, we ask God`s forgiveness and inquire what corrective measures should be taken. On awakening,*

let us think about the twenty-four hours ahead.. We consider our plans for the day. Before we begin, we ask God to direct our thinking, especially asking that it be divorced from self-pity, dishonest or self-seeking motives. Under these conditions, we can employ our mental faculties with assurance, for after all, God gave us brains to use. Our thought-life will be placed on a much higher plane when our thinking is cleared of wrong motives.

George was to tell me that although usually considered part of the eleventh step, that this was the only step I could do out of sequence. He would also point out that nowhere on that page was there any reference to alcohol. George then instructed me to read that page each evening and morning, following the directions in detail. He thought *"any dumb Scotsman"* could handle that task, so I accepted that challenge. I have been doing it so long it is just daily habit, and that suits me fine. I have passed this suggestion along to many along my path. It did work for me, and I am forever grateful.

<u>**STEP TWELVE** – *"Having had a spiritual awakening as the result of these steps, we tried to carry the message to alcoholics, and to practice these principles in all our affairs."*</u>

Living with the Twelfth Step is to experience the joy of living. It is also the result of practicing the previous eleven steps to the best of our ability. We are blessed with what may be described as a ***"Spiritual Awakening."*** For myself, I did not have any great flash of light, with nothing of any great significance happening to me. My efforts at doing Twelfth Step work had been initiated by the prompting of my peers at the many meetings I attended. It involved the making of coffee, opening, and setting up tables for the A.A. Meetings. It also meant chairing of many meetings and becoming the treasurer of my Home Group.

I do not believe it entailed doing a lot of different things, but merely doing a few things a lot of different times. Looking after the newcomers, and speaking with those expressing doubt, seemed to strengthen my own acceptance of what was changing in me. The change in my thought process was ongoing and progressive in a positive manner. I believe the so-called **"A.A. Program"** got me before I got it. My initial efforts were just to suit-up and show- up at meetings daily, acting as if all was well. I began to see my problems of cynicism and skepticism in the faces and voices of others. I was now attempting to provide support and encouragement to those expressing doubts about recovery. Initially, I was somewhat reluctant to admit it to myself. While still having adjustments to make in my way of living and thinking, I was traveling a well-proven path. Becoming a regular volunteer with a willingness to carry the message of hope to the County Jail and State Prison seemed to become my niche in twelfth step efforts. At the weekly jail meeting, I can surely meet my replacement. At the prison, I can look around and think – **"There but for the Grace of God sit I."** I do continue to pursue many avenues, seeking better ways to carry this message of hope. I am convinced that contented sobriety is truly a gift. I feel the purpose of this gift is to help others find their sobriety and peace of mind. My own sobriety is directly proportional to my usefulness to others. It sure seems strange that to keep what we have, we must give it away. Many of the suggestions for living and practicing the Twelfth Step can be found in various writings. I like the quotation from that Irishman – George Bernard Shaw -*This is the true joy of life, in being used for a purpose recognized by yourself as a mighty one. Being a force of Nature instead of a feverish, selfish clod of ailments and grievances. Complaining that the world will not devote itself to making you happy. My life belongs to the whole community, and as long as I live, it is my privilege to do for it whatsoever I can. I want to be thoroughly used up when I die, for the harder I work, the more I live. I rejoice in life for its own sake. Life is no "brief candle" to me. It is a sort of splendid torch which I have got hold of for the moment, and I want to make it burn as brightly as possible before handing it to the future generation.*

My Summary of the twelve steps of Alcoholics Anonymous

It seemed that steps one, two, and three allowed me to quit drinking while not getting me sober. Step four through step nine got me sober, but would not keep me sober. Steps ten, eleven, and twelve, would keep me sober.- Fred H. would tell me - Steps one-two, and three would prepare me for change - Steps four through nine were the process of change. Step ten, eleven, and twelve would provide continuation and growth. I liked that **Preparation -Transformation – Continuation and Growth**

I am responsible...

When anyone, anywhere,
reaches out for help, I want
the hand of A.A. always to be there.
And for that: I am responsible.

"Oh wad some power the giftie gie us - to see oursel`s as others see us"
Eulogy for Eddie Mackay -

He traveled a destructive path, taking life`s gifts and God-given talents for granted.

He did, with reluctant willingness, turn his life over to a God that he had previously abandoned.

He cleared away the wreckage of that past life, making a sincere effort to make amends wherever possible

He Came to Believe in that God of His Experience, trying to live each day by God`s Will, not Eddie`s Will.

He would act like a mature adult and decent human being, while carrying a message of hope to others, with no thought of reward.

He would pray daily to that God of His Experience, asking only for guidance to become more useful to others.

Amazing Grace how sweet the sound - That saved a wretch like me

"Oh wad some power the giftie gie us - to see oursel's as others see us"

About the Author -

Eddie Mackay is a farmer and breeder of Scottish Highland Cattle and Cheviot Sheep. Living in Recovery for 26 years, he remains active in the Recovery Community. While choosing to break personal anonymity, he respects and protects the anonymity of all others in Recovery. Always respectful of Tradition Twelve of Alcoholics Anonymous, which reads as follows.

*" **Anonymity is the spiritual foundation of all our traditions, ever reminding us to place principles before personalities.** "*

If you enjoyed this story, please consider leaving an honest review on Amazon

Resources:-

Dundonald Highlands:- http://www.dundonaldhighlands.com/

Midwest Highland Cattle Association:-

https://www.midwesthighlands.org/

American Highland Cattle Association:-

https://www.highlandcattleusa.org/Default.aspx

Alcoholics Anonymous:- https://aa.org/

Hazelden Betty Ford Foundation:-

https://www.hazeldenbettyford.org/

My Three Lives – So Many Blessings

Amazing Grace how sweet the sound - That saved a wretch like me